INSANITY

Cameron Jace

www.CameronJace.com

Edited by Jami Hampson

Most facts, events, and places in this book sound utterly
absurd, maddening, and fabricated.
They aren't.
Lewis Carroll's personal life facts are true. So is
everything concerning Oxford University.
Every address, name of city, and event are also real. And
of course, the larger-than-life event called *Kattenstoet*.

But then again,
reality is nothing but a figment of our imagination.

How to read this book:

Begin at the beginning
and go until you come to the end;
then stop...

Prologue

Christ Church, Oxford University, Present Day

The girl sprawled on the ground was dead...and loving it. Why else would she be grinning like the Cheshire Cat?

It was early in the morning at Christ Church on the Oxford University campus. A thick mist hovered like veiled ghosts over the quadrangle garden known as Tom Quad. Water trickled steadily from a fountain in the middle like a ticking time bomb. The surrounding buildings loomed behind the cold air like a killer carefully watching the consequences of his brutal crime.

"Do dead people grin, mommy?" a young boy munching on a tart asked a woman in an expensive red coat.

The woman in the red coat was speechless, hypnotized by the grinning girl lying dead on the grass. It was as if the girl was laughing at the living, reminding everyone of their inevitable fates. A breeze of cold air chilled the woman back to reality. She sensed something evil lurking in the mist, so she dragged her son away from the scene of the crime. Some people don't like a murder for breakfast. It's just not their thing.

A few early-wakers stood around the corpse though. None of them questioned the girl's identity, or the significance of the murder taking place inside the college. Again, it was that *frumious* grin on the girl's face that caught them.

"She must be in Heaven, with a grin like that," a senior student joked. He was athletic, not funny, and a typical jerk. The grin didn't conjure happiness. It was sinister, hollow, and nonsensical.

A professor in a tweed jacket knelt down to inspect the body. "It's not a natural grin. Someone did that to her," he declared. "Oh, my God." He looked away from the corpse, cupping his mouth with his hands.

"What is it?" Senior Jerk panicked.

A nerdy girl with thick glasses appeared from the mist, then knelt down next to the professor. "What is it?" she inquired.

"Her lips and cheeks were sewn up with a needle, bearing her teeth to look like she is grinning. It's sick," Professor Tweed said.

"That's bloody gross," Senior Jerk mooed like a cow.

"Look what I found." Nerdy Girl held a tattered copy of Lewis Carroll's Alice's Adventures in Wonderland in her hands. An original library edition from 1865. "The dead girl was gripping it. She had it open to this page."

"What page?" Professor Tweed's curiosity seemed to have cured his nausea.

"This one, where Alice tells the Cheshire Cat she often sees a cat without a grin, but never a grin without a cat. It's highlighted." Nerdy Girl's mouth hung open, locking eyes with Professor Tweed, before they stared back at the grinning girl.

"Is this some kind of sick joke?" Senior Jerk growled, craning his Ogre-thick neck.

"May I see the book?" I said in my raspy voice. I hadn't spoken at all, but I usually like to speak last, after I've heard what else there is to be said.

"Here," Nerdy Girl kindly handed the book over.

I checked the highlighted page. "It's true," I said. "There's also a message scribbled in the margin," I said as I showed it to them. It read: Save Alice!

"Do you think she wrote it before she died, like a clue or something?" Nerdy Girl adjusted her glasses. "Or maybe her name *is* Alice." She rummaged through the dead girl's pockets, looking for an ID.

"I don't think so," I point out the necklace dangling from the dead girl's neck. "It says her name is Mabel."

"I know who killed her!" another squeaky voice popped in from the mist. It belonged to an old woman, hunching over her wriggling cane. "It's the Cheshire Cat!" The few teeth she had left in her mouth chattered.

Senior Jerk chortled. "Are we seriously having this conversation?"

"Don't laugh, young man," the woman struggled on her cane, eager to see the dead girl. "It's all over the news."

"I remember now," Nerdy Girl snapped her fingers. "Cheshire, the Cat. He's killed four girls, until now. Two in London, two in Cambridge, and now it appears that he's killed one in Oxford. All the girls were grinning after they died. I saw it on TV."

"So that's what Alice meant by a grin without a cat?" Senior Jerk mocked them, tucking his hands in his pockets and shrugging his shoulders. Being a jerk is more of a habit or a personality trait of sorts, not an attitude. It's incurable.

"Let me take a closer look at her," the old woman held out a hand.

"I don't think we should be doing this," Professor Tweed snatched the book from my hand, as if I were a lazy student who just got an F in his class. I don't usually tolerate such behavior, but I made an exception. "We're tampering with evidence," he explained.

"He's right," Nerdy Girl leaned away from the corpse. "We should wait for the police. Did someone call them?"

"They're on their way," I replied. "I called them once I came across the corpse."

"So you're the one who found her?" Senior Jerk pointed his big finger at me.

"I did." I always do.

"Why are you grinning then?" he snorted at the same time the professor adjusted his glasses to get a better look at my face. Nerdy Girl shrieked. She bumped against the corpse and fell on her back, not taking her eyes off me. The three of them were in a sudden state of shock. It was the old woman who didn't waste time. She threw her cane at me and galumphed back into the mist, screaming that she'd found the murderer.

My grin widened.

I wondered who I should kill first - Professor Tweed, Nerdy Girl, or Senior Jerk? I'd save the old woman for last. She wasn't going anywhere, running aimlessly across the garden, like in a Caucus Race.

Part One:

We're All Mad Here

Chapter 1

The writing on the wall says it's January 14th. I am not sure what year. I haven't been sure of many things lately, but I'm wondering if it's my handwriting I'm looking at.

There is an exquisite-looking key drawn underneath the date. It's carved with a sharp instrument, probably a broken mirror. I couldn't have written this. I'm terrified of mirrors. They love to call it Catoptrophobia around here.

Unlike those of the regular patients in the asylum, my room is windowless, stripped down to a single mattress in the middle, a sink, and bucket for peeing--or puking--when necessary. The tiles on the floor are black-and-white squares, like a chessboard. I never step on black. Always white. Again, I'm not sure why.

The walls are smeared with a greasy pale green everywhere. I wonder if it's the previous patient's brains spattered all over from shock therapy. In the Radcliffe Lunatic Asylum, politely known as the Warneford Hospital, the doctors have a sweet spot for shock therapy. They love watching patients with bulging eyes and shivering limbs begging for relief from the electricity. It makes me question who is really mad here.

It's been a while since I was sent to shock therapy myself. Dr. Tom Truckle, my supervising physician, said I don't need it anymore, particularly after I stopped mentioning Wonderland. He told me that I used to talk about it all the time; a dangerous place I claim I had been whisked away to, when my elder sister lost me when I was seven.

Truth is, I don't remember this Wonderland they are talking about. I don't even know why I am here. My oldest vivid memory is from a week ago. Before that, it's all a purple haze.

I have only one friend in this asylum. It's not a doctor or a nurse. And it's not a human. It doesn't hate, envy, or point a finger at you. My friend is an orange flower I keep in a pot; a Tiger Lily I can't live without. I keep it safe next to a small crack in the wall, where a single ray of sun sneaks through for only ten minutes a day. It might not be enough light to grow a flower, but my Tiger Lily is a tough girl.

Each day I save half of the water they give me for my flower. As for me, better thirsty than mad.

My orange flower is also my personal rain check for my sanity. If I talk to her and she doesn't reply, I know I am not hallucinating. If she talks back to me, all kinds of nonsense starts to happen. Insanity prevails. There must be a reason why I am here. It doesn't mean I will easily give in to such a fate.

"Alice Pleasance Wonder. Are you ready?" the nurse knocks with her electric prod on my steel door. Her name is Waltraud Wagner. She is German. Everything she says sounds like a threat and she smells like smoke. My fellow mad people say she is a Nazi; that she used to kill her own patients back in Germany. *"Get avay vrom za dor.* I'm coming in," she demands.

Listening to the rattling of her large keychain, my heart pounds in my chest. The turn of the key makes me want to swallow. When the door opens, all I can think of is choking her before she begins to hurt me. Sadly, her neck is too thick for my nimble hands. I stare at her almost-square figure for a moment. Everything about her is four sizes too big. All except her feet, which are as small as mine. My sympathies, little feet.

"Time for your daily ten-minute break upstairs," she approaches me with a straitjacket, a devilish grin on her face. I never get out. My ward is underground, and I'm only allowed to take my break in another empty ward upstairs where patients love to play soccer.

A big muscled warden stands behind Waltraud. Thomas Ogier. He is bald, has an angry-red face and a silver tooth he likes to flash whenever he sees me. His biceps are the size of my head. I have a hard time believing he has ever been a 4-pound baby.

"Slide your arms into the jacket," Waltraud demands in her German accent, a cigarette puckered between her lips. "Slow and easy, Alice," she nods at Warden Ogier, in case I misbehave.

I comply obediently and stretch out my arms for her to do whatever she wants. Waltraud twists my right arm slightly and checks the tattoo on my arm. It's the only tattoo I have. It's a handwritten sentence that looks like a thick arm band from afar. Waltraud feels the need to read it aloud, "'I can't go back to yesterday, because I was a different person then.'" I was told I had written it while still believing in Wonderland. "That Alice in Wonderland has really messed with your head," she says as she puffs smoke into my face and mocks me.

The tattoo and Waltraud's mocking is the least of my concerns right now. I let her tie me up, and while she does, I close my eyes. I imagine I am a 16th-century princess, some kind of lucky Cinderella, being squeezed into a corset by my chain-smoking servant in a fairy tale castle above ground, just about to go meet my Prince Charming. Such imagery always helps me breathe. I once thought that it was hope that saved the day, not sanity. I need to cool down before I begin my grand escape.

Chapter 2

I twist my arms slightly under the jacket to give myself broader space to move. As Waltraud buckles me up, I use one of my hands to inconspicuously pinch the front, and give myself about three inches for slack. I also take a deep breath so my upper body takes more space inside the jacket. I make sure my stronger arm is above the weaker while she pulls the sleeves behind me. When she is finished, I breathe out and feel the gap inside the jacket. People think escaping a straitjacket is impossible. A well-spread myth.

"I feel like throwing up," I lie to Ogier and Waltraud. It's not unusual to want to vomit because of the heavy medications patients gulp all day.

"You're not puking on my uniform like last time. I just had it dry-cleaned," Waltraud sighs in her German accent, the cigarette still between her lips. "Puke in the bucket."

I turn around, happy my trick is working. With my back facing them, I push my stronger arm toward my opposite shoulder. I kneel to the floor and pretend to throw up, as I bring my arm over my head and begin unbuckling the buckle on my sleeve with my teeth. I stretch my back a little and unbuckle the top and bottom buckles behind me. I do it fast, hoping they won't get it. But when I turn around, Warden Ogier has figured out my trick. A big smirk fills his face. He is happy he's found something to punish me for. If I don't act fast, they'll fry my brains in therapy.

In no time, I grab a sedative syringe from Waltraud's pocket and gleefully stab her in the neck, whizzing the sedative into her brain. It works like a charm, but it doesn't stop me from shoving her face into the bucket. I have been wanting to do that all week for the torture she's bestowed on me.

"You little brat," Warden Ogier growls. He holds me from behind by the arms, and lifts me up in the air. I can't free myself. I pull my legs up and flip them backwards until I touch his shoulders. My hands slip from his grip and I start clawing his broad back, like a monkey on an elephant's back. I don't waste time. I pull his prod from his pockets, then buzz him in the neck. He falls to his knees and I follow, standing on my feet.

Dashing out of the room, I hear him moan behind me. He's going to pick himself up in a few minutes. I need to run through the hallways to get to the ward's main door, then escape this nightmare. I need to tell the world that I am not mad — or at least, make sure I am not.

Halfway into the hallway, my feet urge me to a halt. I can't help it. It's my heart that's stopping me, remembering that I have left something precious behind. My Tiger Lily.

Don't do it, Alice. It will stall you. It's just a flower. You only have a minute to run away before the guards know what you've done. Be smart and run away.

I defy all logic and I turn back to my cell. I courtesy-kick the warden in the face, curse him when my leg hurts, push the nurse's face deeper into the bucket, then get my pot holding Tiger Lily. I don't leave my friends behind.

Chapter 3

"Tell me I'm going to be alright," I say to my flower. She doesn't reply. She doesn't nod or flap her petals, or think I am another huge moving flower myself. Good signs. I'm not hallucinating. This is real. I am actually escaping the asylum.

When I am back in the hallway, the patients are screaming my name on both sides. They are pounding on the bars of their cells, trying to stick out their heads.

"Alice. Alice. Alice!" they shout and clap their hands. They are enthusiastic. I could be the first ever to escape the asylum. But they're ruining my plan at the same time, by making all this noise. The emergency siren blares all of a sudden. The guards definitely heard the shouts.

"Get out of here. Prove to them Wonderland exists," a patient in striped pajamas and bunny slippers wails. No wonder she believes in Wonderland. Doctor Tom Truckle told me once that I had great influence on patients, telling them about Wonderland. I don't remember any of that.

"Don't go out, Alice," a woman, holding a pillow as if it were her cat, pleads. "I think the world outside is even crazier than in here."

I keep on running.

The asylum is turning into a mad house. I hear the heavy footsteps of the guards approaching. All I can think of is hiding in the bathroom. I hate bathrooms because they have mirrors, but I have no other choice.

Another patient reaches out his hand from between the bars and grabs me by my gown. He pulls me closer to the bars. He is unlike the rest. He doesn't believe escaping is possible. He has bad teeth, and smells of turtle soup. "Where do you think you're going, Alice?" he whispers in my ear. "You're insane. You belong here."

"Let go of me," I hit him with my elbow and run to the bathroom.

Inside, I shield my eyes with my hands as I dash into one of the stalls, avoiding the mirror. I sit on the stool, holding my pot tight to my chest. Those damn lunatics messed up my plan.

Breathe, Alice, Breathe.

I tap my feet on the floor, contemplating my next move. Then I hear someone singing outside my stall. It's a familiar voice. It has this unexplainable sinister mockery in it. I hate it, but I can't stop it:

When she was good she was very, very good.

And when she was bad, she was horrid.

"Shut up," I cup my ears with my hands. "I'm not insane." I know the voice comes from the mirror. That's why mirrors scare me. But in order to leave the bathroom, I will have to face it. With a drumming heart, I pull the stall's door open. What I see in the mirror paralyzes me, like always. There is a man-sized rabbit inside the mirror. It's white with pink floppy ears. I can't see its features because it has its white hair dangling down in its face. It taps a pocket watch with its fingers, still singing the nursery rhyme. This time it alters a few words:

When she was good she was very, very good.

And when she was mad, she was Alice.

"Tell me I am going to be alright," I plead to my Tiger Lily.

"You're not alright," the flower talks back. "You're insane, Alice. Insane!" It spreads it petals and spits in my face. I am hallucinating again.

The guards bang into the bathroom, and one of them buzzes me with his prod. I shiver and drop the pot, losing my Tiger Lily to the wet floor. When I glance back at the mirror, the rabbit is gone. They will throw me back into my claustrophobic room and probably send me to shock therapy.

As the guards pull me back down the hallway, the turtle-smelling patient sticks his head closer to the bars, shouting at me. "You're not sane, Alice!" He laughs at me and grabs the bars, "You're not. We're all mad here!"

Chapter 4

Doctor Tom Truckle, Director of the Radcliffe Lunatic Asylum, stood mouth agape among his assistants. They were staring at a cell in the VIP ward, where they kept the most dangerous patients. Well, it was only one patient the ward was built for: Professor Carter Pillar, publicly known as Pillar the Killer, one of the world's most dangerous psychopaths.

Unlike Alice's cell, this one was almost as big as a luxurious single room in a five-star hotel. The walls were the color of ripe mushrooms, with all kinds of vintage portraits hung on them. They were mostly portraits of plants and flowers and they made the room look like a forest. The furniture was modern, mostly curvy, with dominant motifs of green and cream colors. It had a refrigerator, a widescreen TV, and a writing desk the color of ravens. Books were piled up in one corner with a couple of tobacco packs on top. A Cuban cigar, a pipe, and dried mushrooms were scattered on the couch. Two lamp stands shaped like bending roses and violets, added a sincere cozy light onto the big creamy couch in the middle, all facing the bars overlooking the hallway where Doctor Tim Truckle stood. A blue hookah stood right before the couch, threads of smoke still spiraling in the air.

There was one thing slightly wrong with Professor Pillar's cell. The professor wasn't there.

"This is a joke, right?" Doctor Truckle growled at the wardens and nurses who were rarely allowed to leave the underground ward—today was an exception, due to the Pillar's disappearance.

The staff lowered their heads, afraid to meet Dr. Truckle's intimidating eyes. Truckle had fired employees for much lesser issues than an escaping patient in the past. The asylum's reputation meant everything to him.

"I think..." a recently hired nurse began.

"You think?" Truckle grimaced. "You don't get to *think* in my asylum. I'll tell you what I think: you're fired."

Immediately, Ogier took her by the arm, and showed her out.

"I don't even know how he does it, Doctor Truckle," Waltraud Wagner spoke slowly. She'd always been among Doctor Truckle's favorites. "The cell is still locked from the outside. There is no sign of breaking out. And he is the one and only patient in the ward."

"Professor Carter Pillar is one of the world's most dangerous psychopaths," Doctor Truckle faced his staff. "He used to teach philosophy at Oxford University, until something happened to him and compromised his sanity," Truckle's eyes widened under his glasses when pronouncing the word "sanity." His thinning blond hair almost prickled, sending goosebumps to his staff's arms. "Pillar the Killer killed twelve innocent people afterwards. The fact that he tricked the court by pleading insanity does not deter from the other *fact:* that he is a cold-blooded serial killer disguising as an insane man." Truckle enjoyed the fear he saw in his staff's eyes. He'd always liked being feared. Otherwise he felt he'd fail in controlling the asylum. "The Pillar might fool you with his charms, hypnotizing drugged eyes, and his nonsensical sarcasm. But if you think his stay here is for treatment, then you're on the verge of insanity yourself. The asylum is more of a prison for him. He's doing time here because neither the Interpol nor FBI could convict him. We're supposed to keep him locked here, to protect the world outside from him." He knuckled his fingers, as if preparing to punch somebody. "So can anyone explain to me how he managed to escape for the *third* time this month?" he screamed from the top of his lungs, his veins protruding on his neck like hot hookah hoses. Most of the staff swallowed hard. There was a saying in the asylum: that the only one madder than a hatter was the Truckle.

"With all due respect, Doctor Truckle," Waltraud said. "I think we should finally inform the authorities."

"You know I can't do that, nurse Waltraud." Truckle gritted his teeth. "We're all going to lose our jobs instantly if we tell them that the man they asked us to simply lock away is gone. Besides, everyone is head-over-heels looking for this Cheshire Cat killer right now. Knowing the Pillar escaped will worsen things for everyone."

"What really puzzles me, Doctor Truckle, is why Professor Carter Pillar always returns from his escape," Waltraud pondered. "I mean, we never report his escape and yet he still returns to his cell, as if it's a walk in the park."

Truckle's face reddened as he stared back at the empty cell. "He's mocking us, Waltraud," he tucked his hands in his pockets and was about to pull out one of the pills his psychiatrist prescribed him. He didn't want to expose himself in front of his staff. If they knew their boss needed help just like any other madman in the asylum, it'd be the end of his career. "He is bloody mocking us, and I am dying to know what he has on his mind," he said, crushing the pill into powder with his fingers. He didn't mind it laying in the bottom of his pockets. He had a lot of pills, as he took four to six a day to calm down.

"Maybe he really *is* mad," Ogier mooed from behind. No one even paid attention to him. "Or why would he always come back?"

"I think it's that Alice in Under Ground book he always keeps with him," Waltraud suggested, pointing at the book that lay on the couch. "I heard he started killing after reading it."

Silence invaded the room, as everyone wondered where Professor Carter Pillar was at the moment.

Chapter 5

Entrance, the Radcliffe Lunatic Asylum

A black limousine halted abruptly before the Radcliffe Asylum's entrance. The recklessness of its driver alerted security at the main gate. They held their guns, squinting their eyes against the framed windows of the unusually long limo. A series of uninterrupted laughter crackled from inside, while the Beatles were playing somewhere in the back. The passengers sang Lucy in the Sky with Diamonds, except that in their version, it was "Alice."

A chauffeur got out and hurried to open the door for his partying passengers in the back. He was so devoted to his job, he hadn't even noticed the security guards with their guns aimed at the limousine. The chauffeur was short. He wore a tuxedo that was too long, as if he'd borrowed it. His face was funny in the strangest ways. It was full of freckles, spattered around a small and pointy nose. A chortle almost escaped one of the security guards upon noticing the chauffeur's thin mustache. It looked more like a rat's whiskers.

The chauffeur cleared his throat, adjusted his necktie, and bent over as he opened the passenger door. Many girls were laughing from inside.

A huge amount of smoke blew into the faces of the guards upon opening the door. It was as if someone had trapped a cloud inside the limo and now it was floating out onto them, like a blob from one of the old scary movies. It was gray, thick, and smelled funny. The guards got a little dizzy.

"Suspicious activity at the main gate," one of the guards dispatched. "Probably tear gas by an intruder. Need backup."

The rest of the guards stood paralyzed inside the big circle of gasses, and waited until it began clearing away. The girls never stopped laughing and cheering for a moment. A few of the guards began coughing though. The first thing the guards saw when the gasses subsided was a girl's leg stepping out of the limousine. It was a slender leg with a tattoo of a caterpillar on it. For guards who'd been handling insane people all their lives, drooling was the least they could do.

Girl after girl got out of the limousine. They wore the tightest outfits, the longest boots, and the shortest skirts. They were either coughing, or giggling. Some of them did both. Most of them were so happy; the guards in the back couldn't help but giggle back. Some of the girls smoked rolled cigars, smiling with kaleidoscope eyes.

It was like a prelude to madness, where the highly respected gangster was about to show up last.

Finally, a short leg showed from the car, followed by the egg-shaped head of a man with a pipe tucked between his full lips. The man's fedora slipped over his eyes as he got out with a hookah in his hand. When he coughed, he vanished like a magician behind spirals of thick smoke. When the smoke cleared, the guards saw he wore a tuxedo with light cream horizontal stripes. His hands were covered in white gloves. His fedora had two spikes that were shaped like mushrooms. Although a bit funny looking from afar, the man had an eerie presence that filled the heart with worry and anxiety. The guards straightened up and aimed at him. They knew the man. It was Pillar the Killer.

Nudging his hat up, the Pillar looked at them with beady eyes. He looked easily content with himself, tremendously annoyed by the presence of others.

"T-turn around. Hands on y-y-your h-head!" one of guards demanded, his anxiety showing in his scattered syllables.

The Pillar, with a hookah in one hand and a pipe in his mouth, looked puzzled. It seemed as if he didn't know what to do with them while surrendering to the asylum's guards. It looked as if someone had awakened him from a drowsy tangerine dream.

"I said turn around. Hands on your head, Professor Pillar," the guard repeated. "You're a fugitive of the Radcliffe Asylum. If you don't comply, I will shoot." It didn't look like the guard was going to shoot. He was bluffing, and scared of the Pillar.

"I was out shopping," the Pillar said. "Needed a purge valve for my hooka-a-a-ah," smoke spiraled from his mouth, hitting the guard in the face. The guard sank to his knees from the power of the smoke and Pillar lowered his head, squinting behind the smoke. "May I ask: *whoo are yooh?*"

Chapter 6

Director's Office, the Radcliffe Lunatic Asylum, Oxford

To meet with the Pillar, Dr. Truckle prepared himself by swallowing two pills at once. His meeting with Professor Carter Pillar wasn't going to be easy. There was a reason behind the Pillar's repetitive escapes. It killed him not knowing it. Pillar the Killer was definitely going to bargain for something. Dr. Truckle had to find a way to compromise with him.

Under no circumstances could the doctor lose his job. It was all he had. After a money-draining divorce, ten years of serving at the asylum and all the secrets the government had buried with him here, he could just not afford it. His kids had just been admitted to Oxford University, and his responsibilities had just doubled. He also had his eyes on the young nurse on the secret ward that hosted prestigious people from the Parliament. Insanity was a disease that spread to all classes and factions.

If the Interpol and FBI had just succeeded in convicting this lunatic Professor Pillar, Dr. Truckle wouldn't have been stuck in this position now. But like always, the small fish had to clean up the big fish's poop.

Giving time for the pills to take effect, he changed the channel on his big screen TV. The news had nothing to talk about but the Cheshire Cat killer. The madman who leaves his victims dead and grinning.

"Boy," Dr. Truckle told himself. "That little Alice in Wonderland book drove the world insane. It's just a children's book, people."

The news showed recent footage of the Cheshire Cat sending a message to the world. It was a head shot, and he wore an orange mask of a grinning cat. It very much reminded Dr. Truckle of his childhood puppy named Garfield—which he loved to snuggle with and nibble at like a mouse. The Cheshire Cat's voice in the footage was distorted, but the words were clear:

"This is a message from the Cheshire to the world. Stay away from me and the people I am involved with. This is beyond the FBI, Interpol, and any other authority in the world. The girls I kill have nothing to do with you. It's a Wonderland War. Stay away. You've been warned."

Dr. Truckle wasn't sure if it were the pills or the Cheshire's monotonous voice that sent a shiver through his spine. The madness he'd just heard on national TV was beyond his years of expertise. It reminded him that the world was mad, in and outside of the asylum. He stood up and adjusted his necktie to meet with the Pillar. But before he did, a third pill wasn't a bad idea.

Chapter 7

When Dr. Truckle entered the VIP ward, Carter Pillar was sitting on the big couch in the middle of his cell. He was still wearing his fedora, white-gloves, and smoking his blue hookah from a pink hose. Dr. Truckle approached the bars while the Pillar leaned over his hookah. The Pillar wasn't an ordinary smoker. He demanded certain sizes, certain manufacturing, and no ordinary ingredients from exotic regions. The professor thought of his smoking as an art. Dr. Truckle was planning to intimidate him with his yelling, but the Pillar spoke first.

"Have you ever wondered if Wonderland is real, Tommy?" The Pillar liked to call him by his first name to provoke him. He didn't even look at him, talking in his distinguished lecturing voice. Dr. Truckle grimaced, suppressing his surfacing anger, unable to respond to this nonsense. "I mean this lovely, stammering writer, mathematician, and photographer named Lewis Carroll couldn't possibly have just imagined Wonderland," the Pillar puffed, readjusting the charcoals with the other hand. "Just think of how his book has inspired, affected, and shaped the minds of children for almost one hundred and fifty years. It's safe to say that Carroll's words weren't a stroke of luck, but of genius. Something in that book makes people relate. Wonderland must be real."

"So instead of talking about your escape, you expect me to talk about Wonderland?" Dr. Truckle inquired, dying to know what was on the Pillar's mind.

"The only philosophical problem with accepting the existence of Wonderland is that it means that our reality could actually be a figment of our imagination," the Pillar puffed out bubbles of smoke, which Dr. Truckle had never been seen before. "An assumption that spikes an even crazier question: Who are you?"

"Listen to me, you piece of..." Dr. Truckle couldn't play along anymore. He fisted one hand, but then remembered to breathe like his psychiatrist advised him. "I don't have the slightest idea how you escape the asylum, but I get your point. You don't really want to escape. In fact, you like it here for some reason. You know I love my job, and could lose it if you escape. So I'm all ears. What do you want in return for your stay, so I won't lose my job?"

"Alice Wonder," the Professor said without hesitation, puffing and adjusting coals. He never seemed to be satisfied with the placement of the coals, as if it were rocket science.

"Alice Wonder?"

"Alice Pleasance Wonder, patient number 1832, the one you lock up in a solitary chessboard-like cell in the underground ward," the Pillar lost his whimsical lecturing voice to a flat and dull seriousness. But unlike Truckle, there wasn't the slightest hint of anger. "The girl you electrocuted over and over again, and succeeded in making her forget all about Wonderland."

"That Alice," Truckle rubbed his chin, pretending he just remembered her. It was a relief knowing the Pillar's need.

"I want you to ask her a question. If I like her answer, then I'd like to meet her in person. Don't send a nurse. Do it yourself, and ask politely."

"You're out of your mind," Truckle spat out.

"'Out of my mind.' Ah, the irony," the Pillar laughed. "My victims used to say that to me." Just like that, any sign of humanity evaded his eyes. The change in his looks was so sudden that Dr. Truckle felt his throat become freezing cold. "I made sure they never said it again," the Pillar added.

The silence in the room suffocated Dr. Truckle. He wanted to disagree, but the Pillar's intimidation was beyond anything he'd done to his own staff. He understood now why the court accepted the Pillar pleading out due to insanity. He was insanity itself. Keeping him away from the world at any price was victory.

"What do you want me to ask her?" Dr. Truckle said.

"It's a simple mathematic question, yet the answer isn't as easy as it seems," the Pillar leaned back on his couch, crossed his legs, and stretched one arm sideways. In Dr. Truckle eyes, he looked like a loony version of Sigmund Freud. "Ask her what four times seven is," the Pillar plastered a fake smile on his face.

"This is nonsense." Dr. Truckle felt humiliated.

"Oh. You haven't seen nonsense yet," the Pillar said. "By the way, I choked one of your guards with my hookah hose and hung him like slaughterhouse meat at the end of the hall. I'd like you to clean that right away, before it begins to smell."

Chapter 8

The Mush Room, the Radcliffe Lunatic Asylum, Oxford

Shock therapy feels like getting high. Each time Warden Ogier pushes the button, my body shivers so hard that my mind goes numb. It's not such a bad feeling, if I think of it positively. I get to shut my mind off to the world for that brief buzz in my body. The world itself seems too noisy to me sometimes.

To top it off, I am soaked in some kind of liquid, so electricity has a more profound effect. Each time he presses the button, Ogier snickers and grins. The shocks are short and to the point. If they send these bolts through my body for a little longer, I might make a good fried chicken dinner for cannibals.

"How does it feel, Mushroomer?" Waltraud puffs spiral smoke in the air. She likes to call us mad people, Mushroomers. This place I am being tortured in is called The Mush Room. It's all the nurses' and wardens' slang. Other than the analogy to most mushrooms being poisonous, they believe shock therapy *mushes* the patients' brains and they find it amusing.

I'm sure Waltraud and Ogier don't want me to die. What would be the fun in that? Watching me suffer is pure entertainment for them. Life underground is pretty boring to nurses and wardens. I can see it in Waltraud's eyes. That's the problem with sane people. They almost always have a license to kill those they think are insane.

"Jeez," I rise against the pain and snicker back at Ogier. "I'm just a mad girl. Nothing personal." I guess I got what I deserved for trying to escape.

Two hours later, I am back in my cell. The pain and dizziness are the least of my concerns. I feel lonely here without my Tiger Lily. Warden Ogier says she's been saved in a newer pot and sent to Doctor Tom Truckle's room, for his own amusement. Poor Tiger Lily, now in the hands of that vicious man.

A few minutes later, Waltraud tells me I have visitors.

Chapter 9

Visiting Hall, the Radcliffe Lunatic Asylum, Oxford

In the visiting hall, I sit opposite my mother and two
sisters. There is no barrier between us. It's just tables. The
visit is a half an hour, max. Radcliffe Asylum's patients
always behave. One threatening look from Warden Ogier or
Nurse Waltraud will suffice.

"How are you, Alice?" my mother reaches out to touch my
hand. I let her, although I am not really sure she is my
mother. She has faint uncombed brown hair. Her eyes are
moistening. I think she loves me.

"Mad." I let out a weak smile.

Lorina and Edith, my sisters, snicker with their hands
covering their mouths. Their eyes are twinkling. They feel
more like stepsisters to me. I don't think they love me at all.

"Don't say that, darling," my mother's sincerity should
affect me. It doesn't. Maybe because I am mad. I don't even
remember her name, so I don't ask. I wonder why I
remember the names of my sisters. Maybe because they are
mean to me. I met all of them a week ago for all I care. Before
that, I was probably someone else entirely. At least the tattoo
on my arm suggests it. "You're just having a rough time."
My mother's still caring enough to make believe she is my
mother.

"Can you get me out of here?" I cut through the drama.

"Here we go again," Edith says. Lorina rolls her eyes and
looks away. I think she's eyeing a cute boy visiting his sick
mother next to us.

I ignore them both anyways. It doesn't look like they'll help
me. "How long have I been here?" I ask my mother.

"Two years," Lorina volunteers back. She looks like she'd like to stick out her tongue at me. "Since you were seventeen."

"And why am I here?" The real question is: "Who in the world am I?" But you can't ask someone that, if you want them to think you are sane.

"You killed your classmates, every single one of them." Edith's words fall like stones on me. I think she is the older one. She is dead serious. Lorina is the flirty one, with an obsession with her manicured fingernails.

"How did I do that?" My brain refuses to believe I am capable of killing anyone. I try to remember anything about it, but I can't.

"See that stare in her eyes?" Lorina tells Edith, as if I am not here with them. "She's in the cuckoo's nest."

"Stop it girls," my mother demands. Although she cares, she looks weak. She has no control whatsoever. It makes me wonder where my father is. I have never seen him. Maybe he is dead, but I don't ask. "Can I ask you a question, Alice?"

I nod.

"Do you still believe that Wonderland exists?"

"No." I shake my head.

"It means your therapy is working," my mother looks pleased. I wonder how she'd feel two seconds in shock therapy.

"What is all this talk about Wonderland?" I wonder.

"When you were seven," Edith's seriousness is annoying. "You went missing one afternoon, and came back saying you'd been to that scary place."

"Edith got punished that day because she was taking care of you, and you escaped her," Lorina can't stop snickering. I understand why Edith is dead serious now. Guilt is eating at her. She hides it by being a jerk.

"Shut up," Edith owns her sister with a sharp look. I wonder how I escaped her when I was a kid.

"Please, girls. Stop it," my weakened mother pleads.

"Why stop it?" Edith says. "I don't buy that she doesn't remember."

"Yes," Lorina backs up her elder sister. "She has to admit the horrible things she has done since she came back that afternoon."

"Horrible things," I tilt my head. "Other than killing my classmates?"

"Remember your boyfriend?" Lorina inquires.

"I have a boyfriend?"

"*Had* a boyfriend," Lorina objects. She seems like she may have had a crush on my boyfriend. "Before you killed him along with everyone else on the school bus two years ago."

"Why would I do that?" It's really hard asking someone else about things you have done, but I truly don't remember.

"Who knows," Lorina rolls her eyes again, snickering at Edith.

"I remember she said something about monsters from Wonderland," Edith laughs back. Her laugh is dull. It's like she's lazy, barely lifting her lips.

"Wonderland Monsters?" I narrow my eyebrows. I am not sure if they're joking, or if that is what I said. Somehow I don't care about all of this. I don't care about my mother's submissive silence, my mocking sisters, not even about the Wonderland Monsters. What I do care about is the boyfriend that I killed. It strikes me as odd. Even with a partial memory, I don't think I would hurt someone I loved. "What's his name?" I ask.

"Whose name?" Edith and Lorina are still laughing.

"My boyfriend, the one I killed."

"Adam," my mother speaks finally. "Adam J. Dixon."

I don't know how or why, but the name Adam J. Dixon suddenly brings tears to my eyes.

Chapter 10

Alice's Cell, the Radcliffe Lunatic Asylum, Oxford

Sleeping has become increasingly hard since I learned about my boyfriend, Adam. It's not like I remember him or the incident of killing my classmates on the school bus. But Adam to me is like Wonderland. I can't remember them, but something tells me they are real.

What bothers me about Adam is that I am strangely mourning his death. I don't know if science has an explanation for my feelings, but I can't escape it. I feel I want to cry for him, visit his burial ground, say a little prayer, and leave roses on his tomb. To me, it's a very genuine feeling. I don't think I even feel this way about my family.

I wonder if it's possible to forget about someone but still experience a feeling toward them. It's as if I have written his name on the inner walls of my heart. As if I am stained with his soul. Whatever we shared is buried somewhere in the abyss of my mind. I just don't know how to swim deep enough and return to the surface with it.

My thoughts are interrupted by Waltraud's knock on the door. Sometimes it feels like I am the only patient in the asylum.

"I am really tired," I say. "I don't want to eat, go to the bathroom, or meet anyone. Leave me alone."

"It's Doctor Tom Truckle," he says, and enters my cell. He has never entered my cell before. When he steps inside, his hands are behind his back. "How have you been, Alice?" He has never asked me so politely.

"Mad." My favorite answer. I think I should copyright it.

"I'll make it short," Dr. Truckle discards my complaint. He looks disgusted with my cell. "This might be outrageously silly, but I really need to ask you something," he shrugs. I have never seen him shrug. He looks uncomfortable with Waltraud's presence. "How much is four times seven?" he asks quickly, as if embarrassed to say it. Waltraud and Ogier try their best not to laugh behind his back.

"Twenty eight," I shrug my shoulders. Then a surge of emotion hits me. It reminds me of my buried feelings about Adam. A light bulb flickers in my head. Suddenly, I realize I know the right answer to the silly question. Whoever told Tom Truckle to ask it of me is sending me a code. I don't know how, but I know. "Wait," I interrupt Dr. Tom's departure. "It's fourteen," I answer with a hint of a smile on my lips.

Chapter 11

"Fourteen it is!" Pillar chirped, coughing some of the hookah's smoke in the air.

"That's the right answer?" Truckle couldn't see the Pillar clearly behind the smoke.

"Indeed," the Pillar said. "Now, bring her to me."

"No. No. No!" Truckle snapped. "That'd be a serious breach in the asylum's rules."

"I've always thought insanity was about breaking the rules," the Pillar said. "Be a good mad boy with a suit and necktie, and bring me Alice Wonder. This just gets better and better."

"What's getting better?" Truckle couldn't hide his curiosity. The Pillar knew how to trigger his buttons.

"Be patient, Tommy. Insane things come to those who wait." The Pillar leaned back on his couch. He looked content. A bit drowsy, too. Truckle remembered a moment in the eccentric professor's trial a couple of months ago. The Pillar had informed the judge that he preferred looking at the world from behind a curtain of smoke. The smoke was like a filtering screen, he had said. It helped him to see right through people's invisible masks.

"I suppose I can make an exception and get her to meet you briefly," Truckle considered. "But only if you tell me—"

"I know, I know," the Pillar waved his gloved hand in the air. "You'd like to know why four times seven is fourteen. The answer is actually buried somewhere in your own childhood, Tommy, but let's say you can find it here." He nudged a copy of Lewis Carroll's original Alice's Adventures Under Ground toward the edge of the cell. Truckle was going to reach for it through the bars, but pulled his hand back.

"Oh," the Pillar said. "You're scared to even reach in. How very sane of you," he smirked. "Rest assured, Tommy. In Lewis Carroll's book, there is a part when Alice wonders if she's hallucinating. She questions her own sanity, and if she's even Alice at all."

"What?"

"In chapter two, The Pool of Tears, Alice tries to perform multiplication, but produces some odd results. She does it to assure herself she isn't mad," the Pillar said. "Alice finds out that while she is in Wonderland, four times five becomes twelve, and four times six is thirteen, and four times seven is…" the Pillar's eyes glittered, looking at Truckle.

"According to this nonsensical logic, fourteen." Truckle felt ashamed at having said that, but he wasn't good at caging his curiosity.

"Frabjous, isn't it?" the Pillar waved his hands like a proud magician.

"So this is some nerdy code for those obsessed with the book?" Truckle expected more than this. The professor was a killer for God's sake. What in the world was his interest in children's books?

"Nerdy is an awfully racist and out of fashion word," the Pillar raised his forefinger. "We call ourselves Wonderlanders."

"Are you kidding me? You sound like you believe that Alice Wonder is *the* Alice in the book," Truckle chortled. "You're the optimum zenith of insanity. I don't think I can even profile you."

"It's time insanity has a role model," the Pillar dragged long enough on his hookah to make a whizzing sound. "Now, go get me Alice, before I change my mind and escape again."

Chapter 12

On my way to meet this mysterious Professor Pillar, I break free from the warden and run toward Tom Truckle's office to get my Tiger Lily. My attempt is overruled again as the wardens grab hold of me and tie me back up in a straitjacket. This time, they squeeze me in hard, so I can't untie myself.

Ogier grins, watching me buckled up. He taps his prod on the thick flesh of his palm, as if reminding me how much he'd enjoy shocking me if I untie myself again. As they walk me up to the VIP ward, I try to squeeze my head for deeper memories of Wonderland and the people I supposedly killed. I can't remember anyone, not even the Pillar who wants to see me.

"You're by far one of the worst Mushrooms in my asylum," Dr. Truckle says, adjusting his tie as he walks beside me. He's always been self-conscious about the fancy way he dresses and how he looks. But it's the first time he calls me a Mushroom. "And even though you killed your classmates, I know you're not a naturally born killer. I have been treating you for some time, so I know what I am talking about." He stops before the metallic door leading to the VIP hallway. It looks much cleaner than the mess I live in downstairs. I think of it as purgatory, one step away from the sane world outside. "Like I told you, Professor Carter Pillar is a cold-hearted murderer. He's done horrible things, like pulling his victim's eyes out and stuffing their sockets with mushrooms. He used laughing gas on another victim, and smoked his damn hookah while watching him die of internal bleeding caused from the laughter. He even once hypnotized a man and made him jump off a rooftop of the Tom Tower in Oxford University after persuading him he had wings."

"What's your point, doctor?" I can't help but notice Truckle's uneasiness with the Pillar. It makes me curiouser and curiouser.

"The point is… once you're alone with him, he is known for messing with people's minds and convincing them of any ideas he wants to seed in their brains," Dr. Truckle says. "He always has an agenda, and knows how to read through people's insecurities. I advise you to stay tied in your straitjacket and as far away as possible from the bars of his cell. Or you'll jeopardize your chances of leaving the asylum."

"I didn't know I had a chance in the first place." I stare him right in the eyes, making sure he isn't lying or playing games.

"I know it's crazy, but you do," Dr. Truckle laces his hands together. "Your mother's lawyer has convinced the court that if the asylum proves you've been cured, they will rule out your crimes of killing your classmates."

"She did that?" So the woman with the name I don't know must be my mother after all.

"She's been trying with all her might to help you," Dr. Truckle says. "If that happens, then you've committed the perfect crime in my opinion; killed your classmates, pleaded insanity, got cured, and got your freedom afterwards. That must be every teenager's dream." He continues, "To believe you're cured, we have to either make sure you're not fooling us when you say you don't remember Wonderland, or..."

"Or?"

"Or the Pillar proves you're sane." Dr. Truckle rubs his chin.

"How would a madman, serial killer, who dresses as if he is a caterpillar, prove that?"

"By proving that Wonderland is real." Dr. Truckle's face suddenly changes, and he begins to laugh at me as he nudges me through the door. I guess he was just messing with my head.

Chapter 13

Tied up in my straitjacket, I walk down the hallway to meet with this Pillar. It's a much cleaner and broader hallway than mine downstairs. All cells are empty. All, except the one with a shimmering yellow light. I hear faint music playing in the background. As I walk closer, I recognize the tune. It's White Rabbit by Jefferson Airplane. Smoke circles out of the cell as I stop in front of it, ready to meet him. Pillar the Killer himself.

The Pillar's cell is luxurious in a mad way. Its floor is levitated almost a foot above the hallway's floor. It makes it look like a performer's stage. The Pillar is sitting, legs crossed, on a huge couch. He is smoking his hookah with one hand and holding a jar with a butterfly inside with the other. The butterfly crashes against the glass, wanting to be set free. The Pillar doesn't care.

Silence creeps into the place and I don't feel like starting the conversation. The Pillar's eyes scan me in a most unusual way. It's as if he knows me, has known me, and is making sure it's really me. Although mad people don't intimidate me, I feel mysteriously uncomfortable. He has such an unexplainable presence for such a short and average-looking man.

There is a chair in the hall facing the cell. I sit on it, not taking my eyes off him. His eyes are beady as he waves the hookah's hose in the air. He does it like a maestro orchestrating the song's unusual melody. It takes me a while to discover he is writing words with his hookah's smoke in the air. The smoke magically sticks. It's a question, one that may have been easier for me to answer more than a week ago: "Whooo are you?"

This isn't happening, right? This is too surreal, even for my insanity.

"I'm not sure who I am," I say, wondering why I feel the need to comply. "People around me seem to have an idea of who I am, though."

"Who do they think you are?"

"They say I killed my friends." I raise my eyes and stare in his, realizing that in the weirdest of ways, we're both killers.

"Why haven't I ever thought of that?" he sucks on his hookah.

"Think of what?"

"Killing my friends," he puffs a ring of smoke back into the room. "But then again, you can't kill something you don't have."

"You don't have friends?" I didn't except him to open up to me. Or, is he?

"Neither have you."

"Actually, I do."

"Ah, you must mean your Tiger Lily. A very interesting species," he sounds either sleepy or too comfortable in his skin. An apocalypse wouldn't shake him off his hookah. "I heard you messed up your escape because of it."

"She is the first thing I remember seeing from a week ago. Since then, she has been my only friend."

"I wonder if it meant more than that in the past." The Pillar takes a long drag.

I stop and think about it. Was I attached to it because of an older suppressed memory, maybe? "Is that why you wanted to meet me, to ask about my flower?" I wonder.

"Of course not. I am here to talk to you about Wonderland."

"Then you better read the book," I'm tired of talking about Wonderland. "Because it doesn't exist in real life."

"That's strange. I am quite sure your mother and sisters repeatedly mentioned you talking about Wonderland. A real one." His eyes pierce through me. I am not even going to ask how he knows about my mother and sisters.

I am not comfortable with him knowing about my family, but something makes me keep talking to him. "My mom says I escaped from my sister Edith when I was seven, and came back blabbering about a scary place called Wonderland," I say. "It's a crazy story. I think it was my childhood imagination after reading Alice in Wonderland. It's just silly."

"What's life but a big silly book?" he says. "You've answered the question I sent you. It means you must remember something."

"I don't know how the answer came to me, but I assume it's because it was written in Alice in Wonderland."

"No, it's not. The fact that four times seven is fourteen is only hinted at in the book. It's never mentioned. You remember more than you think you do, Alice. It's just the shock therapies and medicine that made you forget," the Pillar says. "Seriously, Alice. Aren't you curious about the things you don't remember?" He places his hose on the edge of the hookah and leans forward. It's the first time he gives me his full attention. "I can make you remember amazing things."

"Like what?"

"Like who the Red Queen really is. Why she chopped off heads. Who the Rabbit really was. Where the real rabbit hole exists. What a raven and a writing desk really have in common. Why Lewis Carroll wrote this book. And a lot of the other things," the Pillar says. "Basically, I can tell you who you really are. And you know what happens if you know who you really are?"

"No, I don't." I think I am better off not knowing who I really am. I don't know why I think so.

"You get to know if you really killed your classmates. And if you did, you get to know why you did it." The Pillar stops for effect. I am almost sure of what he will say next. "Don't you want to know why you killed the boy you loved?"

Chapter 14

The Pillar's last remark gets to me the most. I still can't shake my mourning over the boy I loved but can't remember. Adam and my Tiger Lily seem to be all I care about in this world.

"I am listening," I say. "Tell me what you want."

"I want him," he says without hesitation as he clicks his TV screen on. It shows news coverage of the Cheshire Cat murders.

"You're not going to tell me this is the real Cheshire Cat, are you?" I chortle.

"What do you care? Wonderland isn't real to you, correct?" he smirks. "I will guarantee that you leave this asylum twelve hours each day, see the world outside, do the little tasks I ask of you, and then come back and sleep in the asylum at night."

"That's not possible. The judge says I am insane. It's official."

"I believe you noticed I have an effect on Dr. Truckle. Trust me. He will do as I say."

"I assume these tasks have something to do with catching the Cheshire Cat?" I raise an eyebrow. This conversation seems surreal to me. I am not sure if I am not just hallucinating it.

"If you do as I say, we'll catch him," the Pillar says. "Don't worry. I won't ask you to shoot a gun or be in great danger. You'll just help me solve some puzzles about him, and then go to bed like any obedient mad girl."

"You realize this should be the police's work, right?"

"Trust me, they can't catch him. Besides, wouldn't you feel better if you helped in catching him and saving tens of other girls from getting killed?"

I like the idea, although saving people isn't something mad girls should be doing. "And what will I get in return, other than the chance of seeing real sunshine and snow for the first time in the last two years?"

"I am hoping that at some point you'll remember Wonderland again and I can prove your sanity. But I know you're not enthusiastic about this idea," he says. "Tell you what; I can make Dr. Truckle get you a cell like mine."

"I don't care about the cell," I say. "For my first mission out, I want my Tiger Lily back."

"The Tiger Lily again," he considers.

"And a bigger source of sunshine for it to grow in my cell."

"I like a girl who knows what she wants. We have a deal," he says.

I nod, not knowing what I am doing exactly. All I can think of is that I will get out of this place, even if it's for a few hours a day. I wonder if I will get to go watch a movie or go out and eat ice cream, like normal people do. "Deal," I say.

"Frabjous," the Pillar chirps. I find it silly that he uses this word, but I also find it amusing.

"How do we start?" I ask.

"Why don't we start with that silly straitjacket of yours? I heard you're a master of escaping it."

Part Two:
We're All Mad Here

Chapter 15

VIP Ward, the Radcliffe Lunatic Asylum, Oxford

The next morning, they send me back to the VIP ward. I'm surprised no nurses or wardens are present. Instead, the hallway is filled with Mushroomers from another ward.

"Welcome to the pinnacle of insanity," the Pillar waves his cane in the air, like a circus ringmaster. He hasn't started smoking yet. I guess it's too early, or maybe he prefers to sober up while I am on this mission. The mad patients dressed in their tattered gowns, surround me with giggling eyes. I feel like I am in an insane zombie movie, the princess of all zombies. "Aren't you going to greet your fellow lunatics--or should I call them 'colleagues?'" the Pillar says, throwing parental glances at them. They seem to adore him.

How did he even get them out of their cells?

"What are they doing here?" I try to keep a stride or two away from the nearest *fellow*. I was thinking today was going to be my first day to mingle with normal humans. I guess I was wrong about that.

"The nature of your mission is highly secretive," the Pillar explains, patting a mad girl who hugs him tightly, as if he is the Easter Bunny. "I mean, maddeningly secretive. You're going to deal with the Cheshire Cat himself, a most wanted criminal Wonderlander." He excuses himself from his fangirl. "This means no *sane* person can be part of this." He air quotes the word "sane."

"And if anyone asks me what I am doing?" I say.

"Anyone, like who?" he wonders.

"Police for instance?" I tilt my head.

"Didn't you listen to the Cheshire's footage, explaining that this is a Wonderland War?"

"Yeah, right." I purse my lips.

"Alice, Alice, Alice," he sighs. "Here is how I look at it. In order to prove you are sane, you will have to do insane things. Think it over before you accept my offer. This is truly like a rabbit hole: once you fall in, there is no coming back."

"You mean none of the nurses or wardens are even going to know?" I thought I could get Waltraud and Olgier to treat me better at least.

A mad Mushroomer laughs with puffy eyes at me and wiggles his forefinger into a "no." He has a crooked big finger he could wipe windshields with.

"But Dr. Truckle knows," I remark, avoiding the Mushroomer.

"Oh, Tommy," the Pillar says. "I consider him one of us," he points at the patients. "He's just good at hiding it, fooling the universe that he is a sane man running an asylum. Isn't it so, Mushroomers?" He addresses the patients, who nod eagerly.

I rest my case.

The Pillar signals to a few of his Mushroomers to bring something. They arrive with a walking wardrobe on wheels, one that wasn't here before. They pull it in front of me and point at it with drooling mouths. I'm now Alice, princess of fools.

"Harrods?" I read the name on the wardrobe. "You bought me clothes from Harrods?"

"I'm not sure we *bought* them," the Pillar exchanges glances with them. "But they're here, aren't they? Insane people have to get dressed too." The patients nod at me.

I let out a long sigh, then breathe all the sanity I can think of back in. Before arriving, I was offered a nice shower in the underground ward. Waltraud and Ogier thought I was going to be examined by a highly regarded specialist outside of the asylum, where I'd be exclusively supervised by Dr. Truckle. I understand now that Waltraud is going to stay oblivious to my secret mission. But it's alright, who can resist a wardrobe from Harrods?

I rummage through it and end up choosing dirty blue jeans and a white t-shirt. A girl in tattered clothes flashes her thumbs at me, liking my choice of clothes. I can't help it, and toss her a dress out of pity. She looks at it for a moment, not knowing what to do with it, and ends up chewing on it.

The Pillar tells me that it's lightly snowing outside, so I throw on a light blue pullover with a hoodie and long white sleeves. An older Mushroomer woman throws me white boots and giggles at me. Gotta love them loons. They're all I got, after all.

"Look at you," the Pillar looks happy. "A modern day Alice. Lewis would have been proud."

Although I don't have the guts to stare in a mirror to see how I look, I feel really fresh. I'm not sure if it's the clothes, the freedom, or my loony friends. But here I come Wonderlanders.

The Pillar's fangirl passes me a pink watch. It's beautiful.

"I was going to get you a golden pocket watch, but then I faced some obstacles," the Pillar says.

"Couldn't steal from the guys at Rolex?" I chuckle, putting on my watch.

"Problems with Wonderland rabbits actually. They are the watchmakers, and control the industry all over the world," the Pillar mocks me. "Caterpillars and rabbits don't get along, you know." The Pillar turns to look at a couple of Mushroomers working on a typewriter on his writing desk in his cell. They are typing furiously and debating about something. One of them types, the other pulls the bar to start a new sentence. They stare at it, as if it's an atomic bomb. I peek in to see what this is all about. They keep gluing and cutting papers with scissors.

"Are we done, or what?" the Pillar puffs impatiently. I am wondering what this is all about.

One of them walks out of the cell with an old camera. It's a 19th-century style camera with bellows for focusing. He places it on a tripod in front of him and asks me to pose. I am still puzzled.

"Say 'cheese' Alice," the Pillar demands. "The Mushroomers have no use for technology and smartphone cameras. They must've been here since long ago," he rolls his eyes.

I smile flatly at the Mushroomer taking the picture. As fast as a rabbit, he hops back to the writing desk and continues writing and cutting with his friend. He returns with a card in his hand and a drooling grin. It's a pretty smile, actually. Insane, but truly and outrageously happy. I am starting to envy the Mushroomers.

I'm not going to ask how the Pillar knows about my mirror phobias. I assume he knows more than I know about myself.

Seeing my face in the card is a better solution than looking in the mirror. I've never thought about it. I like the way I look. I have auburn hair, naturally wavy—or is it just an after-effect of too many shock therapies? I have light blue eyes, and a slightly edged face. You can tell I don't eat much, I guess. My skin is fair, and I have an overall ordinary and familiar face. If I hadn't been in an asylum, I could have been someone's neighbor, girlfriend, or college girl in a small town.

But that's not what this card is about. When I read it, I discover it's an Oxford University card. It has my name on it: Alice Pleasant Wonder. I am a freshman.

"It's Pleasance, not Pleasant," I tell the Pillar.

"Pleasant is more *pleasant*," he says. "Besides, you're not an Oxford University student either. Don't be picky when it comes to forging."

"You're right about that. I'm just silly," I note. "I haven't even finished high school."

"Oh, you have *finished* that," he laughs. "How many did she kill again?" He addresses the Mushroomers. They start jumping and clapping, and his fangirl grabs my hand and raises it, like a winner at a boxing match. "She finished all her schoolmates, didn't she?" The Pillar is overly content with having mad people around him. It's a totally different side of him that I don't think he shows to the world outside. "Now it's time to catch a killer, and save some lives." He rubs his hands together and walks back to his couch in the cell, and starts smoking his inverted mushroom-shaped pipe.

Chapter 16

"Are you ready?" The Pillar says.

"I'm not sure, for what?"

"It means you're ready. Shall we start?" He pushes a copy of Alice's Adventures Under Ground toward me, as I stay right behind the bars. The copy isn't his. It's an old library edition, and it has a girl in a yellow dress on it.

"I always thought Alice wore blue," I comment, picking up the book.

"False myth number one," the Pillar says. "John Tenniel, who drew all of Lewis Carroll's paintings in the book, depicted Alice in a yellow dress in the first released version in 1865."

"You're not serious, are you?"

"I am insanely serious. From now on, everything I say about Wonderland is dead serious, Alice."

"Why yellow?" I glance at the cover again.

"Yellow was considered the color of madness at the time," the Pillar explains. "But let's not get lost in such debatable details now," the Pillar says. "Flip through the book, and tell me what you see."

"A regular Alice in Wonderland paperback," I tilt my head, then flip through it. "It's a library copy. It has a British library's stamp on it."

"Good," he nods. "Where is the British library located?"

"In London?"

"Right. What else do you see?"

"Someone borrowed this book yesterday," I can see the date on the inlaid card. "I didn't know libraries write borrowing dates inside their books."

"They don't," the Pillar explains. "Someone wants us to know the date. What else do you see?"

"There is a map tucked between the pages. It's old, and it looks like it's been drawn by hand. A map of Oxford University." I unfold it. "A place called Christ Church, to be exact. One location is circled in red," I stop and resist the peak in my pulse. The read circle has the face of a grinning cat on it. "Is the book another message from the Cheshire?"

"It is. What does it say under the cat with the grin on the map?" the Pillar doesn't waste time.

"It says: 'We're All Mad Here.'"

"Clichéd to the bone, isn't it?" the Pillar smiles faintly.

"There is an arrow pointing to a location underneath. What is all that? I don't understand."

"That's Cheshire the Cat's most recent message," the Pillar says. "He is playing with open cards now, knowing you and I are in the picture."

"Should we be looking for something where the arrow points?"

"Indeed," the Pillar puffs. "You're going to follow that trail today."

"I am? I thought it's my first day at college," I say.

"College sucks. First days, especially suck. Saving lives doesn't."

"Who said anything about saving lives?" I inquire. "It's just a map. I am assuming it leads to a treasure or something."

"You're wrong. This book was found in the hands of another dead girl this morning."

"What? Different than the one he killed in Christ Church two days ago?"

"Yes. In London, next to the British library. They're going to announce it on the news later. For some reason, he left evidence to show the girl is dead, but took her with him."

"Is that his way of mocking the world, sending messages with dead girls?"

"In his case, he is grinning at the world. He wants us to discover something in that location he circled," the Pillar says. "I believe it's another girl he has trapped somewhere."

"Why is he killing those girls? What does he want?"

"I have no idea what he wants with the girls. But I think he is also testing you, Alice."

"Why would he test me?" I feel anger seeping through my pores.

"He wants to know if you're the real Alice," the Pillar's gaze is stripped of any emotion.

I consider all the possibilities of who I really am for a moment. Then I dare the Pillar's eyes back, "You realize it's my first day among sane people," I say, thinking about what I am getting myself into.

"If you've survived parasites and bacteria until the age of nineteen, you can survive sane people." He draws on his pipe.

"But you realize this is bit too much for me. I don't want to end my first day being called insane in the sane world."

"You're caring too much about people, Alice," he says. "Take it from me: sane is mundane, insanity is the new black."

I can't even smile at his absurd comment. Saving someone is a big responsibility. I am not sure I can save myself. All that I can think of is this: "What would the real Alice do?"

"Save the girl, of course."

Chapter 17

When Tom Truckle opens the asylum's door for me, I shield my eyes from the sun. Although weak against the snow, its rays feel hot on my face. We haven't met for so long, I guess that's why.

My legs are stiff as the cold breeze outside licks at my face, like an unfriendly dog. The idea of facing the sane world again isn't as exciting as I would have thought. I feel like I am missing the dim-lit corridors and the crazy faces of patients. Watching people walking around me in suits and coats just doesn't feel right. I wonder if evolution wasn't from ape to man, but from insane to sane.

I take a deep breath and step outside. The sound of the door closing behind me echoes in the back of my head. I feel disconnected, left alone in this new world. I find it ironic, wanting to escape the asylum before. If the wardens only knew I'd feel so intimidated. I wonder if that is why the Pillar always returns. Is it possible he couldn't make it among the sane, so he began killing them?

I walk to the first bus station with books in my hands. I haven't even looked at them. It feels good standing among people and waiting for a bus though. No one knows I am insane. No one cares who I am. I hope it's going to be easy fooling them into thinking that I am one of them. One of the privileges of not knowing who you are is that you can pretend to be anyone you like.

Getting on the bus, I pay for my ride to Oxford University, which isn't that far from the Radcliffe Asylum—people outside call it the Warneford hospital. I guess they're embarrassed to say "asylum." Money feels funny in my hands. *If I give you this slice of paper, you let me on the bus?* It's ridiculous.

I pick a seat by the window in the last row, and sit. I'm used to sitting with my back against my cell's walls. Last rows suit me fine. I make sure I don't pull my knees to my chest and bury my head in my hands, like I usually do. It reminds me that I am lonely out here without my Tiger Lily.

I don't know how I'd feel if someone sits next to me. Proximity with others doesn't sound like a good idea right now. I haven't sat close to someone for a long time. I'm not even sure I am capable of having a regular conversation with anyone. What if they ask me about a street address? What if they ask me what I am studying, or who I am? I glance at my books. They're mostly psychology and philosophy books. One of them is a children's novel though. It's called: There is a Mad Girl at the End of this Book. It makes me laugh. I take it that it's the Pillar's doing.

My phone buzzes. I look around, as if I am doing something wrong. Everyone's phone buzzes. I am just not used to it. I pick it up. It's a message from the Pillar. Next to a mental health hotline, he is the only one on my contact list. The Pillar doesn't stop playing with me.

"Doing alright?" his message reads.

"A little uncomfortable with being around people," I write, having a hard time typing on the phone's small touch keypads.

"Do you see a rabbit with a watch, late for an appointment?"

"No." I giggle, and I think people notice.

"Then you're alright. You're a psychology student with exceptionally high grades in high school, in case someone asks you."

"Why psychology?"

"Most serial killers and criminals study psychology at some point. It's easier to spot them that way," he writes. "I want you among them."

"Did the Cheshire Cat study it?"

"Definitely. Tell me, what do you see around you, Alice?"

"Trees, pavement, and people walking outside my window."

"And the passengers on the bus?"

"Normal people. I see an old woman who just bought some groceries. A young couple, probably heading to the university, too. A middle-aged man with a suitcase. He looks like a professor. And a few other regular people."

"All sane?"

"I take it this is a joke," I smile as I write. "How do I know?"

"Sane people care too much about silly things, Alice," the Pillar writes. "Is the professor checking his tie and jacket, maybe the suitcase? Does he look insecure about his looks?"

"He is checking his tie actually," I write, and look around to see if the Pillar is on the bus, but he isn't.

"The couple. Are they holding hands? Do they look worried, not comfortable with others seeing them together?"

"No. They are chatting casually," I write.

"Does one of them react more to the other? Look harder, Alice. Is one of them talking, making more of an effort to please the other?"

"Yes," I write. "But that's normal. Why are you asking?"

"I'm not asking. I'm teaching you how to spot Wonderland Monsters. They don't have these human emotions and insecurities. A Wonderland Monster's face is void of life. For instance, if you meet the Cheshire Cat, you'll know him from his grin. It will be an empty grin, void of these simple emotions you notice about the people on the bus."

"The Wonderland Monsters look like normal people?" I write.

"At this time in history, yes. They are reincarnated in normal looking humans. It doesn't make them sane or friendly, though."

"That's reassuring :p."

"Oh, you still remember emoticons. Where are you?"

"Close to Christ Church, like the map indicates. Should I get out there?" I write, making silly conversation. Having him on my phone isn't a bad idea. He keeps me company.

"Exactly. Once you reach St. Aldates Street, watch for the bus station closest to the Tom Tower, one of the college's most important entrances," the Pillar says. I remember Dr. Truckle saying the Pillar made someone jump off the Tom Tower. "If my timing is correct, the bus should be stopping there in about five seconds," he interrupts my thought.

The Pillar is right about the timing. I wonder how. The bus stops at St. Aldates Street. It's a beautiful entrance to Christ Church's College. A couple of students beat me to the door, as my stiffened legs are pondering if I really want to do this. I shrug, and it feels like I have a lump in my throat. Stepping out of the bus feels like a big commitment to catch a crazy killer.

Suddenly, a boy bumps into me from behind. "Don't act like a tourist," he whispers in my ear. "Or they'll figure out who you really are."

His voice sends a strange shiver to my soul. A good one, although I can sense he's arrogant and too sure of himself. Before I turn around to look at him, I notice he smells of playing cards.

Chapter 18

St. Aldates Street, Tom Tower Entrance, Christ Church, Oxford University

It's not the most amazing smell, but it reminds me of old books and things as ancient as human souls. The boy pushes me ahead to get off the bus with the other students. I don't have a chance to tilt my head and see his face.

"Goodbye, fat, old, and obnoxious bus driver, whatever your name is," he salutes the driver and nudges me off the bus as it hits the road again. I am surprised the bus driver doesn't slam back at the boy's rudeness.

On the ground, I turn around and flash my angry face at the boy. Something I am very good at. "Who the heck do you think you...?" All of a sudden, I can't speak. The boy wears a hoodie like me, and he has this peculiar smile. Peculiar in what way, I can't put my finger on it. It's like a soft smirk of mischief that is softened by the dimples on both cheeks. It makes him look familiar and oddly trustworthy. I can't yell at him. I wonder if that's why the bus driver took his insult lightly.

As the moment freezes, the boy looks down at me. A strand of black hair dangles on his forehead as he hangs onto his backpack. It's a funny bag, with all kinds of playing cards glued to it. They're all Jacks of Diamonds. I guess that's where the smell comes from. It's really silly. It doesn't match his good looks.

"Wow, girl," he breaks the silence. "We're not even going to kiss yet. I need comfort, dates, and little cuddling before I go there."

"What?" my face tenses. I can't seem to shake off what people around me say. I feel insulted by his remarks. Did I really get lost in his attractive face that much? "I don't even know you."

"After all we went through on the bus?" his eyes widen, and he cups his mouth with one hand. "I was so close to dying for you. All you had to do was ask."

"You'd die for me?" I blink my puzzled eyes. "You just weren't ready to kiss me?"

"So you changed your mind about the kiss," his smirk is like the devil, his dimples are angelic.

"Urgh," I sigh skyward, almost fisting my hands.

"You don't have to get his permission," he acts puzzled, looking at the sky above. "Jesus must have kissed somebody."

"Jesus?" My face is red, I wonder why I am not just walking away from the embarrassment.

"Jesus," he repeats. "The guy who saved the world and looks as good as me."

"This is nonsense!" I freak out. Should I tell him I just left an asylum? Damn my feet. Why am I not walking away?

"I love nonsense." He pulls his hood back, and holds me by the arms. "You know there is an actual science to it?"

My phone rings. It's probably the Pillar.

"Oh, you have a boyfriend?" the arrogant boy says, as I am already checking it.

"No," I can't remember which pocket in my jeans I tucked the phone in.

"Awesome!" he rubs his hands.

"I mean yes," I find the phone in my back pocket. I feel guilty not mentioning Adam. Why in the world do I feel like that, if I don't remember him?

"Bugger," the boy pouts, and I realize I don't want him to leave.

"I mean, no."

"Oh," he tilts his head back. "You're not insane, are you?"

I don't answer. My tongue is tied, then I push the green button to answer the Pillar.

"His name is Jack Diamonds," the Pillar says on the other line. "He's a big distraction. Get rid of him. We don't have time."

"But..." I don't know how to explain my curiosity about Jack to the Pillar. Before I even ponder the thought, a number of students rush out from another bus and I find myself pushed through the main entrance with them. When I tiptoe to see Jack again, he's gone.

Chapter 19

Garden, Christ Church, Oxford University

"Right now you're walking under the famous Tom Tower," the Pillar plays my tourist guide on the phone. "It was designed by Christopher Wren, who was also the architect of St. Paul's Cathedral in London."

"Alright?" I remind myself that I am on a mission, and that I might never see Jack again.

"The Tom Tower is a major tourist attraction. I can spend all day long telling you about it. One thing is that it houses the Great Tom, the loudest bell in Oxford."

"Do I have to know about this?"

"Everything I tell you is important, Alice. You might not use it now, but later," the Pillar is back in his lecturing mode. "The Great Tom bell is sounded 101 times every night, around five past nine, Oxford time. In the past, it was used as a curfew alarm, to remind students to get back to their dorms. Also, somewhere up there was Lewis Carroll's own photography studio."

"Lewis Carroll was a photographer?"

"And a mathematician and painter, among other things. The guy was a genius. He even predicted Einstein's theories in a paragraph in his other book, The Hunting of the Snark."

I am very curious about his photography. "What were his pictures like?" I don't know why, but something tells me I have to see the photos.

"They were of girls mostly, but we'll get to that later. Focus only on everything I tell you, Alice. Everything is important," the Pillar insists, as I walk through the huge cloisters.

I get inside Christ Church College and look at a huge green area in front of me. The college is a fortress, a quadrangle of Renaissance buildings encompassing the green garden in front of me from four sides. There is a fountain in the middle of the garden. The scenery makes me forget about Jack. This place has an unprecedented presence. It's like it holds great secrets; like great men and women have walked its earth.

"I see you went speechless," the Pillar says.

"I can't explain it, but there is something about this place that feels so..."

"Mad?" the Pillar amuses himself. "It's one of the most mysterious places in history. Mad people know that. Sane people think it's just a college, where you get a degree and hang it on the wall. Walk around for a minute, Alice. Let it sink into your soul. Breathe the same air Lewis, and many other geniuses, breathed centuries ago. By the way, you should use your headset, since I will be in your ear for the rest of the day."

"That's reassuring," I purse my lips, then put my headset on.

"That's better. Here's a brief history of this frabjous place," the Pillar says. "Christ Church is one of the largest colleges in the University of Oxford. It has a world famous Cathedral Choir, a most respectable library, and a unique and very old cathedral. Let alone, the many untold secrets it keeps safely from the sane people of this world."

"I'm listening." It's true. I wonder why I haven't read about it before I arrived. I am already enchanted by it.

"Over the years, Christ Church has had many distinguished students, tutors, and visiting academics. In my eyes, they are the most amazingly insane men of history. To name a few: madman and philosopher John Locke, madman and scientist Albert Einstein, more than thirteen madmen British prime ministers. And of course, our most beloved madman of all, Lewis Carroll."

"He went to Oxford? I thought he only used the place above as a studio."

"It's almost an insult not to know that, Alice. He was a math tutor at Christ Church."

I come across a temporarily closed area. The police are all over the place. Students can only pass by showing their IDs, and having their bags inspected.

"I assume you've arrived at the crime scene by now," the Pillar says. "Where the Cheshire killed a girl, a professor, a jock, an old woman, and a young girl two days ago."

"How do you know that?" I look around, to see if he's watching me nearby.

"You're very predictable, like most people, Alice," I can hear him puff his pipe. "You'll have to learn to be unpredictable if we want to catch the Cheshire Cat. Now walk ahead toward the police, and don't look too long at the crime scene. A regular student should have seen it before."

I approach the policeman. I can't help but shrug. It's not like I am a criminal. I am afraid he knows I belong to an asylum and will put me back in. I just can't help it. I mean, the cold oxygen I am breathing here still feels like a dream.

"Alice Pleasant Wonder," the police officer reads my name on the card. "A lovely name."

All I do is smile. I hope I come across as sincere and normal.

"It reminds me of the girl who killed her classmates two years ago," he says.

My heart sinks to my belly.

Chapter 20

The Great Hall, Christ Church, Oxford University

Time stops, and I have no idea what to do. I can't seem to utter words until the police officer speaks again, "Except that, that Alice's last name was 'Pleasance,' and she's in an asylum."

"Yeah, I always get that." My smile is plastic, but he doesn't notice. Now I know why the Pillar changed my name. Although trivial, it makes me someone else. Did the policeman really fall for that, or do I smell something wrong?

"You look perfectly sane to me," the officer says. I notice he tries to act serious, but he looks funny. He has a peculiar moustache, thin like a mouse's whiskers. "Have a good day."

"Thank you." I take the card back and take a couple of steps up into the building.

"Liar, liar, pants on fire," the Pillar chirps in my ear.

"That wasn't funny."

"It wasn't supposed to be. Anyways, what you're entering now is the prestigious Great Hall."

The Pillar's words ring in my head as I enter this enchanting place. Long dining tables are stacked on both sides. They are filled with all kinds of dining instruments, bowls, forks, and placemats. Gold and brown are the most common colors in this yellowish, dim-lit place. The walls are unusually high, and majestic in ways I can't describe. Portraits are hung behind the table on both sides. Exquisite oil painted portraits of people I don't know.

"A unique place, isn't it?" the Pillar says.

"Unbelievable." I am enamored.

"The Great Hall is where they filmed movies like Harry Potter. All that abracadabra wizard nonsense couldn't have used portraits if the Great Hall didn't exist," the Pillar says. "Also, movies like the Golden Compass with its hodgepodge white bears were filmed here. The Great Hall is where every great story wants to take place."

"Really? I never knew that. Why do I sense resentment toward these movies in your voice?" I can't help but take the chance and ask him. The Pillar doesn't open up. Seeing him personally irritated at something gives me a small window into his mind.

"Why do I resent them?" the Pillar wonders. "Alice. Go ask any tourist about the Great Hall, and they always mention this Harry Potter, but never Lewis Carroll and Alice in Wonderland. Harry Potter isn't even real. Lewis and Alice are."

"I assume by Alice, you mean me?"

"Let's not get ahead of ourselves. You will know everything in time."

I walk further into the hall. "So why am I not in class, and here walking around the Great Hall?"

"Pull out the map from the book. What do you see?"

I do as asked, and stare at the Cheshire Cat's map. It doesn't take a genius to see this is the circled spot on the map.

"Make sense now?" the Pillar says.

"It does." I fidget in my place. Looking around, the magnificent place turns into a scary castle in my eyes. What if the Cheshire Cat is watching me now? What if this is a trap, and I will be dead next?

Chapter 21

Inside the Great Hall, I walk among tourists. I didn't know tourists from all over the world visited during college hours, but I like the idea.

Everything around me is grand and majestic. I come across a table full of empty teacups right before the Great Hall's massive door. "What are those teacups for?"

"They are usually for professors' and intellectualists' meetings," the Pillar says. "Rarely are they for the priests from the cathedral, who sometimes have special meetings in here too."

"Don't tell me the Mad Hatter is involved?" I don't know how I even dare to ask.

"Be careful of what you wish for, Alice," the Pillar's says. "He's even worse than the Cheshire. Are you inside the hall yet?"

"I am."

"Tell me where the arrow on the map points exactly. Can you make it out?" the Pillar demands.

"It points at the portraits on the wall behind the tables in the Great Hall."

"These are portraits of very respectable men and women you're staring at, except they aren't wizards," the Pillar chews on the words. I think he really hates Harry Potter. "Well, they are real wizards of science, literature and all sorts of arts. Can you tell me which portrait the Cheshire Cat wants us to see?"

"Hmm..." I count the portraits on the map. "It should be...let me see..." I walk tangent to the wall, and finally stand in front of a black and white portrait. It's of a middle-aged man, with fair features and nurtured hair. He looks very familiar. Very intelligent. I read the sign underneath, "Charles Lutwidge Dodgson."

"Interesting." I hear the Pillar breathe into his pipe. "So that's what the Cheshire want us to look at."

"Who's Charles Lutwidge Dodgson?" I say.

"Shame on you, Alice," the Pillar laughs. "It's Lewis Carroll's real name. It's written right under the name on the plaque."

"Lewis isn't his real name?"

"Lewis Carroll is a pen name, part of the forgery of the truth behind Wonderland," the Pillar says. "Let's figure out why the Cheshire wants us to look here. It's one of his games, I'm sure. There has to be a reason behind it."

"Maybe he's just fascinated with Lewis Carroll?" I suggest, unable to see something peculiar in the portrait.

"You still think this isn't the real Cheshire Cat, and just some infatuated copycat?" the Pillar says. "You're even worse than the media. Look harder at the portrait. Something must be odd. The Cheshire likes riddles."

I look, but I can't see anything that catches my eye. I even check the portrait's frame, to no prevail. A couple of tourists glance awkwardly at me when I do that. "Could you just tell me what I am looking for?" I whisper, aware of a few people around me probably thinking I am mad, talking in the headset all the time.

"It depends on what you want to find," the Pillar muses.

"That's not funny."

"I think it is. Tell me, Alice. Lewis's picture is a profile, right? Do you see anything in the direction he is looking toward?"

"Another portrait. Einstein."

"Does he still look crazy with that white cotton candy-like hair?" the Pillar mocks him. "Anyways, I don't think that the Cheshire want us to look at Einstein. How about the portrait opposite to Lewis's on the other side?"

I turn around. "Actually, there is no portrait in that spot on the other side. You think it's a secret door?"

"Let's not get ahead of ourselves. It's unlikely that the answer is that far from the location of the portrait," the Pillar says. "Since the portrait faces the table, do you see anything unusual on the spot facing Lewis Carroll?"

"I do," I say. "It definitely unusual, but it I don't think it belongs to the Cheshire."

"Can you please describe it?" I sense the Pillar's curiosity in my ears.

"It's a block of cheese," I try to sound casual. Why is there a block of cheese in the Great Hall?

"Cheese. How quaint," the Pillar laughs. "Of course, I don't have to tell you what cheese and a grin have in common."

"I suppose you say 'cheese' when you grin in a picture, which refers to the Cheshire Cat somehow?"

"He has a sick surreal sense of humor, doesn't he?"

"He has a sick mind. He kills young girls. Besides, it says Cheshire Cheese on the block."

"Cheshire Cheese. Now that's clever," the Pillar snaps his fingers.

"I don't see how."

"Lewis Carroll was born in Daresbury, Warrington, in Cheshire," the Pillar says.

"Is that a coincidence?"

"From now on, there are no coincidences. Everything we'll go through is preciously planned by the Cheshire, and its solution has to relate with Lewis Carroll."

"Is that what inspired Carroll to create the Cheshire character, because he was born in the town of Cheshire?"

"Create, no. Write about, yes," the Pillar explains. "Cheshire is a dairy county, long known for a peculiar cheese warehouse in the banks of the river Dee. That's when it was still a port, more than a hundred years ago."

"So?"

"Patience, my dear mad girl." The Pillar pauses and takes a longer drag on purpose. He wants to teach me to listen, and not interrupt him. "Of course, a cheese warehouse in Cheshire attracted a whole lot of miserable rats." He imitates their squeaky voices on the phone. I am starting to glimpse part of his insanity. "The rats came from all over the world to the cheese warehouse, thanks to the ships arriving to transport the cheese. That's when the cats crawled into Cheshire County, assembling on the dockside to catch the endless amount of rats. And since no Pied Piper ever came to Cheshire, the Cheshire Cats were the happiest in the kingdom. Happiest means they grinned all the time."

I find myself wanting to sit all of a sudden, still staring at that grinning cat on the block of cheese on the table. Part of the Pillar's story sent thunderbolts to my head, as if I should remember this myself, but I can't. Another part was the craziness of the fact that the Cheshire Cat is real. This isn't a game. This isn't a copycat.

"Alice?" the Pillar says.

"I'm here. Just felt a bit dizzy. Why is the Cheshire sending us this message then?"

"Well, for one, the message is for me. I imagine he has other riddles for you, later. As for now, he wants to remind us he is real, not just a grinning cat in a book with pictures. He has a history and an origin. He wants us to respect him."

"So what is he? A cat possessing someone's soul?" I let out a nervous laugh.

"I can't answer that now. But you'll never look at cats the same way again, will you?" the Pillar laughs without acknowledging me. "Now, let's get back to the puzzles. Look closer at the block of cheese. You might find something underneath it. I'm sure this game isn't finished yet."

I pick up the cheese and inspect it.

"Anything?" the Pillar asks.

"Yes," I say. "When I turn the cheese upside down, I see something carved on its back."

"Please read it, Alice. Meow some Cheshire music to my ears." The Pillar is a notch too excited now. I'm caught between a serial killer I am supposed to catch, and another puffing nonsense in my ears.

"It says: Eat Me." I shake my head at the silliness.

"Now that's frabjous in a very Jub Jub way," the Pillar claps his hands.

"Look, I'm not going to do it," I fist my hands and whisper with gritted teeth.

"I think you will, Alice," the Pillar says in the calmest voice I've ever heard.

"Listen, you little piece of..." I wave my forefinger in the air, and notice people tilting their heads toward me. "You little piece of caterpillar," I smile broadly at the tourists. They squint at my absurdness.

"Poor girl. She's caught into the act that she really *is* Alice," an old woman with white bushy hair tells her husband. "She even dresses like her."

"Wise woman," the Pillar laughs at me on the phone.

"The tourists think I am a loon," I turn and face Lewis Carroll's portrait, so I can talk to him privately.

"Good for you, or they'd be calling the police for suspicious activity in the Great Hall. Now be a good girl, and do what the Cheshire asks."

"Tell me one reason why I should, Professor Pillar," I challenge him. "You can't make me."

"Please look at the back of the Cheshire's map, and then tell me you have changed your mind." He is too sure of himself. No hint of sarcasm or insanity.

I pull the crumbled map from my pocket and flatten it upon the portrait. The heck with what people think of me. I flip it on its back and discover there is handwriting in the middle: *Either you solve my riddles fast, or the next girl dies before noon.* The message hits me like a pebble in the eye. I raise my head and gaze at the sun beyond the high windows. Its rays are almost perpendicular outside. I have so little time to save a girl from death. The sneaky Pillar knew about her from the beginning.

"Still think you're not mad, Alice?" the Pillar's voice scares me. "Because it rather takes a mad to catch a mad."

Chapter 22

"Give me a minute to think it over." I turn around and stare at the big block of cheese.

"A minute might be a bit too late," the Pillar says. "Look at you, staring at the cheese like a hungry mouse. The Cheshire is probably watching you somewhere, and his plan is working so far," the Pillar's words tick in my head like a time bomb. A girl's life is at stake here. "I hope you get the irony he is conveying. Back in Cheshire County, he used to feed on the mice eating the cheese from the warehouse. By eating the cheese, you will be his little mouse now, Alice. Your reluctance isn't doing the girl any good."

"Alright. I'll take the cheese to the bathroom and cut it open with something," I pick it up from the table. "I assume there is another message inside. Like a fortune cookie, maybe."

"Alice, Alice, Alice," the Pillar sighs. "When the Cheshire says 'eat me,' you have to eat it. You don't have time. Just look at the sun." I tilt my head again, and see his point. I can't believe a girl's life depends on me. Who in the world am I to save a life? "Come on, pull your sleeves up, and dip into the cheese. Detach yourself from the tourists. What's the worst that could happen: they might think you're insane?" the Pillar is having the time of his life.

And I have to save a girl whom I don't even know.

I take a deep breath and close my eyes, then sink my teeth in the cheese. It's actually delicious. I nibble on it at first, as the people around me gather to see what kind of cuckoo I am. I have no time for them. Maybe I'll have time to explain later, after I save the girl.

The nibbling turns into bites. I choose a side and bite through, waiting for a piece of paper to come my way. It doesn't.

I turn the block of cheese and bite the other side. I am trying my best not to even breathe. The sun has turned into a bomb, and keeps on ticking in my head.

More people gather around me, staring at the nineteen-year-old in a modern Alice dress gorging on cheese.

A boy picks up the Cheshire's label which has fallen from the block, and shows it to other people. "It says: Eat Me!" he laughs. "This is so awesome!"

I am biting from a third side now. I can't see the sun through the glass anymore. It's going closer to perpendicular. Or am I just panicking?

Tick Tock. Tick Tock. I think I am going to vomit.

"It's a show." The old woman with the white bushy hair is back. "She isn't a crazy girl. It's a show, and it's entertaining!" She begins clapping, and the tourists follow. They don't clap as in "wow, that's awesome." They clap as if we're in a beer fest, and I am doing the polka dance.

I take a deep breath and sink in again. My head is going to explode. Why is my head ticking louder whenever I eat more chunks? I can't find the Cheshire's message. This must be cheese overdose.

"You think she'll grow taller?" another tourist asks.

"Nah," her husband says. "That's the kind of stuff they'd do in Disney."

Tick. Tock. Tick Tock.

"Interesting how mad behaviors always entertain the sane," the Pillar whispers in my ear.

"Shut up!" I yell at him, spitting Cheshire Cheese on the tourists.

They clap even harder.

"Tell me, Alice," the Pillar says. "Why is your head ticking?"

What? How can he hear the ticking in my head? Now, this is absurd.

"It's like Tick Tock, all the time," the Pillar says. "Do you have a time bomb somewhere?"

I can't believe he hears my own thoughts. I can't live this way if he truly does. Suddenly, my teeth hurt really badly. I have bitten something made of steel. My eyes widen, as I keep chugging through the cheese like chattering teeth. The message isn't a piece of paper. It's something made of steel. Finally, something falls off the cheese. A watch.

"That's why I thought I was ticking," I mumble. The tourists laugh. They're on cloud nine now.

"A watch?" the Pillar wonders. "Please tell me it is not a pocket watch, or this Cheshire's sense of humor is atrociously absurd."

"It *is* a pocket watch," I pick it up and rub the cheese off it. "It has a rabbit drawn inside. His two hands show the minutes and the hours."

"That's brilliant. Show me!" the old woman says.

"Don't you dare come near me," I sneer at her, and get back to the Pillar. "The watch isn't working. It stopped once I touched it, I think."

"That's even more interesting," the Pillar says.

"Do something!" I shout at him. "We have to save the girl."

"Don't yell at me. I am not the killer here," he says. "Well, I kill people, but not this one. Tell me Alice, anything unusual about the watch?"

"Other than that it's not working, I don't think so."

"A pocket watch that isn't working," the Pillar thinks aloud. "What time is it stuck on?"

"Six o'clock."

"That's the message," the Pillar says. "I don't really know what it means, though."

"What? How can you not know? I thought this was some kind of sick game you were playing with the Cheshire. You have to know."

"I don't," the Pillar says firmly. "Sorry, kid. We're going to have to give up on the girl. It's almost noon, and the Cheshire wins this round."

"I'm not going to give up on her!" I shout.

"Why? You don't even know her. She means nothing to you," he says.

I say nothing, because I don't know why. I just have to save her. I can't stand knowing that I could save someone then bail on them.

"Did the Cheshire eat your tongue?" the Pillar says.

"Okay, okay," I try to calm myself down. The tourists are taking pictures of me. They are filming me with their phones. That old woman keeps grinning at me. "Let's see. The watch is fixed on six o'clock. Now it's around twelve-thirty. The Cheshire said I have until noon, so six o'clock can't be a number. It can't be time."

"Interesting," the Pillar says.

"It's a location." I raise my hands in the air. "Like snipers and policemen in movies, when they say shoot this one in the six o'clock direction."

"Frabjous," the Pillar says. "And where is six o'clock as a location?"

"Right behind me," I turn around, back to Lewis Carroll's portrait.

"Like the Cheshire used to say: if you don't know where you're going, any road will get you there," the Pillar says.

Chapter 23

It doesn't matter how long I inspect Lewis Carroll's portrait, I don't find anything strange. It's devastating. Even the tourists start to get bored, all except the old woman. She is most attentive.

"Tell me Alice, does Lewis Carroll grin in the portrait?"

"No." I double check, in case my eyes are giving up on me. I had one shot of my medication early this morning. I might need another one, since I'm beginning to tire.

"Damn. That would have been classic," the Pillar says.

"Maybe it's something behind the portrait," I suggest.

"I know what six o'clock might be!" the old woman interrupts. Her grin is ridiculous. She is enjoying this more than a seven-year-old would enjoy an Alice in Wonderland book with pictures.

"Okay?" She might be my last resort.

"Six o'clock is when the Mad Hatter froze time by singing in his awful voice. The Red Queen said that," she says.

"The lady is actually right," the Pillar speaks in my ear.

"So what?" I wonder. "What's the Mad Hatter got to do with this?"

"It might not be a direct reference to the Hatter. What is the Hatter famous for?"

"Tea, his hat, and mad parties," I reply.

"That's the answer," he says, but I don't get it.

"I think it could be the teacups in the entrance of the Great Hall," the old woman suggests. "Wherever the Hatter goes, there are teacups." I don't even know if she knows what's going on. She thinks this is some kind of interactive assembly by Oxford University to entertain the tourists, I guess.

"I always thought Lewis Carroll's books were suitable for nine to ninety-year-olds," the Pillar says. "She isn't over ninety by any chance, is she?"

"Shut up." I dart across the hall, pushing the tourists away. I catch the eyes of a security guard, but he doesn't approach me. I wonder if he knows about me.

I arrive back at the entrance with the huge table with plates and tens of empty teacups on it. I check each and every teacup.

"She's Alice Bond," the old woman claps her hands.

"All cups are empty. All but one," I tell the Pillar.

"Does it say 'drink me'?" the Pillar says in his whimsical voice.

I don't even waste time. My fingers reach into the tea in the cup, and they touch something. Here it is, just what I was looking for.

"It's another watch… digital," I say.

"Working?" the Pillar asks.

"No."

"Rub it like you'd rub a bottle with a genie in it," I hear him take a drag. "I'm sure it will start counting downwards."

"Why?" I rub it with my sleeve anyway.

"The last watch in the cheese was ticking, and it probably stopped when you rubbed it. This one will work once you rub it. It's just the kind of nonsense the Cheshire would insure."

"But the time was fixed on six o'clock then. He couldn't have predicted when I'd rub it," I say.

"A watch can still when its hour and minute hands are fixed, Alice. It's not that hard to understand. Now, rub this one."

I do. The Pillar is right. It's a stopwatch. The clock's digital counter starts counting backwards. Six minutes in, I tell the Pillar.

"So we have only six minutes left. A new deadline," the Pillar comments. "Tick. Rewind. The madness begins again."

Chapter 24

"There must be some other clue in the teacup, because this is definitely the last mile in the puzzle," the Pillar suggests.

The old woman pulls a folded piece of paper from the cup with that silly grin on her face.

"A paper," I unfold it, and read it to the Pillar. "It says: '*a four letter doublet.*'"

"That's what I call exciting," the Pillar says. "What else does it say?"

"There is a drawing of a door, then an arrow that points from the door to a drawing of a lock," I say. "What the snicker snack is a doublet?" I have no idea why I am talking in the Pillar's slang all of a sudden.

"A doublet, also called a 'word ladder,' is a game invented by Lewis Carroll during the Christmas of 1877," the Pillar lectures. "It's a simple game. I tell you a four-letter word, and ask you to turn it into another word by changing one alphabet at a time."

"What?" my head is frying. I can't even focus on the game.

"Let's say I ask you to turn the word 'Word' into the word 'Gold.' First, you'd change 'Word' into 'Wood' by changing one letter, then you'd change 'Wood' into 'Good.' Then finally, you change one last letter in 'Good' and turn it into 'Gold.' Easy Peasy, if you ask me."

"So what's this got to do with saving the girl?" I glance back at the watch. Five minutes.

"The Cheshire drew a door and a lock for you," the Pillar explains. "He wants you to turn the word 'Door' into the word 'Lock.' And since I know how crazy he is, I imagine this is somehow your clue to unlock wherever the girl is being kept. Behind some door, probably. Better get going, Alice."

"Okay," I panic again. The old woman's eyes widen. I am not sure if she heard the Pillar, but she encourages me and tells me I can do it. "Let's remove one word from 'Door.' Let's change the 'R' into an 'M.' 'Doom.'" I snap my fingers.

"No. Alice, no," the Pillar says. "You can't *see* 'Doom.' It has to be something you can see or work with where you are. Each word that will come up will help you find the real lock."

"'Door' into 'Boor?'" I mumble.

"Sounds good," the Pillar says.

"What's a 'Boor?'" I wonder.

"A person of rude and clumsy manners. Go on. You're on the right track."

"Now we change 'Boor' into ... hmmm ... 'Book?'" I raise a finger in the air.

"Excellent. I imagine we could find a useful book nearby. Go on."

"'Book' into 'Look?'" I'm improvising.

"And finally, change a single letter in 'Look' and you get 'Lock.'" The Pillar claps. "Well done."

"And then what?" Four minutes left.

"Look around for a boor, Alice," the Pillar says. "Come on. You don't have much time. A boor. Listen hard for a student, a professor or a tourist who is complaining, obnoxious, and ill-mannered. There are plenty of those in the world."

"A boor who is unpleasant and rude," I remind myself as I look around.

"My husband is definitely unpleasant," the old woman says. "He is in the next hall, arguing over the price of a book he just bought."

"A boor and a book. Two for the price of one," the Pillar nags me in my ear. "And it's not even Christmas yet."

Chapter 25

"Sir," I call to the man, running toward him.

He stands arguing with the librarian that he has to refund him because the book he bought has holes in it. When I arrive, I find out that this part of the hall has been emptied for cleaning. The staff members are asking him to leave as it needs to be maintained. I whiz through and don't let anyone stop me. They stop his wife from following me though.

"I paid for this book," the obnoxious man protests. He looks just like I had always imagined Ebenezer Scrooge from A Christmas Carol would look in my mind.

"Please, Mr. Scrooge," the librarian pleads. "We need you to leave the hall."

I don't even let my mind consider the fact I heard his name is Scrooge. I find it too distracting, and I have a girl to save.

"Please, Mr. Scrooge," I plead. "Could you please show me the book?"

"Of course not," he is a tall scruffy man, and pulls the book away. "I bought it, and it's mine."

"You have only three minutes," the Pillar reminds me. "You have to get that book. It's part of the Cheshire's puzzle."

"Please, Sir," I plead again.

"So it's a valuable book, eh?" Mr. Scrooge glances at it one more time with a smug look on his face. The book is about Lewis Carroll's life at Oxford University. "How much would you pay for it?"

"Pay?"

"Bugger," the Pillar muses. "Now you have to get a loan from the bank to save the girl. I think it takes between three and four weeks to clear. Not too shabby. You could save the girl's corpse by then. Besides, I don't think the banks give loans to girls with a record of madness. They know girls are shopaholics."

"Shut up!" I yell.

"You're telling me to shut up?" Mr. Scrooge frowns. "That's it. No book for you, young lady."

"I'm sorry. I didn't mean it that way. Listen, I can give you this," I show him the six o'clock rabbit watch. It looks expensive, even classic.

"A watch?"

"It's not just any watch. It is Lewis Carroll's own watch. See, the rabbit? It's even six o'clock all the time, just like when the Mad Hatter sang and froze time."

Mr. Scrooge tilts his head and inspects the watch for a long time. His gaze is penetrating. His eyebrows arch, as if he is a British minister about to take a crucial decision. He glances back at the book, then at the watch. Time is running out.

"You want this book for this watch?" he says.

"Yes, please." This must be the hardest bargain I have ever had to make.

"You got it, young lady," he hands me the book and laughs. "She wants this book so badly," he mumbles as he walks away. "It's full of holes," he leaves the hall. A security guard comes and shows him out, then nods at me. He has that silly pointed nose and a face full of freckles. He is the same person who pretended to be the officer asking for my ID. Before he pulls the hall's door to a close, he tells me, "Do what you have to do. Fast!"

"It's nice to know someone is helping," the Pillar says.

"Who is that, and how does he know me?"

"He works for me."

"And where are the real guards?"

"Sedated and bound somewhere in the Tom Tower," the Pillar says.

I know I should object, but all I can think of is saving the girl. There are certainly no morals whatsoever when working with the Pillar.

I get on my knees and inspect the book. This fits the sequence; first the 'boor' who turned out to be Mr. Scrooge, then the 'book' about Lewis Carroll, and then 'look' inside the book.

"I'm looking inside the book. I imagine that should send me to the 'Lock,'" I tell the Pillar.

"Are there any messages from the Cheshire on the first page or the cover?"

"Yes," I almost laugh when I read it. "It says: What is the Use of a Book, Without Pictures or Conversation."

"And?"

"The answer is: holes."

"I assume the book you have has holes in it, like Mr. Scrooge said."

"Yes. The book has two big holes on each page," I tell the Pillar.

"What shapes are the holes?"

"They look like two tall rods, thicker at the bottom, and thinner as they stretch up. They have two heads at the ends that look like some kind of soldier with an unusual hat, I think. It could be a plate on their heads."

"I see." The Pillar's voice dims. "Damn that Cheshire. He was really playing with us from the beginning."

"You know what that is?"

"If you're sitting, raise the book and look through at the East Wall." I do as he says. "You should come across two brass firedogs in front of a fireplace. My guess is, if you stay right in the middle of the room at that level, you'll see they fit the cut size in the book"

I do as he says, and he is right. I see the brass firedogs. They're gold plated and very unique. In fact, they remind me of Lewis Carroll's Alice in Wonderland right away. I don't know what it is, but they carry his sense of nonsense and humor.

"What are they supposed to mean? I don't see a 'lock.'" I feel out of time, and disappointed.

"You like the firedogs?" a voice sneaks up from behind me. I thought I was alone in the hall, or is it one of the Pillar's assistants? When I turn around, it's Jack Diamonds.

Chapter 26

Jack has his backpack on one shoulder, and his curly hair falling down his forehead again. And of course, that attractive smirk.

"What are you doing here?" I snap.

Jack closes his eyes and puckers up his lips, as if we're about to kiss. "You owe me a kiss."

"What? You're out of your mind." I can't even imagine this guy is for real. "How did you even get in here?"

"I'm a dangerous man," he opens his eyes and shapes his fingers into what makes them look like a gun. He starts to shoot like a cowboy. "Wanna go out on a date?"

"Ugh," I sigh. He is certainly a distraction. Where did he come from?

"Doesn't have to be a date then," he changes his mind. "I could drive you around Oxford in a limousine, and be your chauffeur for one night."

I shake my head. I wonder how the Pillar knows Jack. "Do you even own a limousine?"

"No, but I will steal one for you, buttercup," he pulls me closer from my waist so fast, I can't even shake myself free. "My name is Jack Diamonds, by the way." He whispers softly in my ear, "I'm a thief of hearts. Pun intended, of course."

"Let go of me," I say as I pull away.

"Wow, you're good at squeezing yourself away from a man's arms," he looks admiringly at his empty embrace.

"You haven't seen me with a straitjacket." The words spill out of my mouth spontaneously. It takes me a second to realize that I can't let him know I sleep in the asylum at night.

"Straitjacket?" He raises an eyebrow, "I didn't know you're into bondage and stuff."

"Get rid of him," the Pillar says. "I told you he is a distraction."

I stare at the watch, and gaze back at Jack.

"Why are you always on the phone? He tilts his head and flashes his boyish dimples. Too boyish for a twenty year old. "Are talking to that old man who just walked out? You're not dating him, are you?"

"Shut up." I have one minute left, as I look back at those brass firedogs. "What about the firedogs? I have no time." I squeeze my headset, talking to the Pillar. I'll have to work, even if Jack is still behind me.

The Pillar abandons me.

"You don't need a date, buttercup. You need a tour guide," Jack spreads his arms and bows his head, as in "I'm at your service." "The firedogs are Lewis Carroll's inspiration for the long neck chapter, when she eats that cake and gets taller."

"Really?"

"Yeah, she keeps getting taller and shorter, and taller and…"

"I know the book," I wave my hand in the air. "This is how the Cheshire was fooling us from the beginning." I click my fingers together, pretending Jack isn't here. "When he wrote 'eat me' on the Cheshire Cheese, he was referring to the girl's hiding place," I tell myself, interpreting the last piece of the puzzle. Suddenly, I shriek. "It's the fireplace! He's locked the girl behind the fireplace!"

Thirty seconds left.

"There is a girl behind the fireplace?" Jack looks puzzled as I run around, looking for anything to help me bring down the brick wall blocking the fireplace.

"A big hammer will do, Alice," the Pillar decides to talk to me again. "Faster. Go get help from outside! They'll know how to break it."

And just before I run to the door, I hear the bricks falling in a series of consecutive thuds. I turn around, and see Jack bringing down the brick walls with the firedogs. He has strong arms, and he is determined as heck. He also looks like he has a thing for vandalism.

"The heck with national treasures!" he pants, as the bricks fall down.

I pass the firedogs and squeeze myself in the tight place behind them. Then I get on all fours and use the phone's light to peek into the darkness of the fireplace. I smell ashes, but can't see anything. Then I hear a girl moaning. I don't hesitate, and crawl into the dark.

It doesn't take me long before I can see the shadow of a girl inside. She's lying on the floor with her hands and knees tied.

Chapter 27

Oh, my God. She's only ten or so. I run to her and get on my knees. I have to crawl inside to get to her. Her mouth is tied and her dress is torn, ashes covering her legs. The look in her eyes is killing me. Those pleading eyes. I can't imagine she's been locked in this awful place for so long. This damn Cheshire Cat. I swear I will catch him.

When I reach my hand for the girl, she pulls away, still panicking. I'm assuming she is in great shock. "It's alright," I say. "I am here to help you."

The girl stops panicking, but doesn't move or allow me to untie her hands and legs. I feel like I want to scream and cry at the same time. I want to tell her that I know what it feels like, being trapped and isolated in such a small room. She reminds me of myself in the asylum. I am praying the Cheshire didn't do this on purpose, sacrificing the girl to play with my head.

Whenever I crawl closer to her, she shies away. I don't want to force her. She's been through enough. I need to find a way for her to trust me. I reach for the ashes and smear them on my face and hands, trying to assure her we're both alike. That I can save her, only if she'll let me. The girl still doesn't trust me. Her mouth is duct-taped, so she can't speak. But her eyes speak. I wonder what she wants to tell me.

"Please, let me help you," I plead, tears trickling down my cheeks.

She does that thing with her eyes again, unable to speak.

"At least let's remove the duct tape, so you can tell me what you want."

She thinks about it, then nods. I crawl over and pull it slowly. She's brave. She doesn't moan anymore.

"Are you Alice?" she asks me, with her faint and weakened voice.

"I am." There is no point is asking her how she knows now.

My answer makes her relax. She allows me to unbind her and help her crawl out of the fireplace. We get out to the middle of the hall, where she hugs me while I am on my knees. Then she finally lets go, and cries hysterically. She's been through a lot.

My whole world is falling apart. I have never felt this much emotion for such a long time--I don't even know how long. The sane world is too cruel, I think as I hold her tighter to me. I don't even know her, but I want to give her all the love I can provide. How can the Cheshire do something like that to this young kid? The sane world is horrible. The Pillar was right. Living among the sane is insane.

"I'm not a fan of drama," Jack says from behind me. When I tilt my head, I see him climbing out of one of those highly arched windows. Is this guy some kind of a thief, or what? "But you owe me a date!" he points a finger at me, then waves goodbye to the girl. I am surprised she waves goodbye to him. For the first time, she smiles.

When I turn to look at Jack again, he's gone.

"Well done, Alice," the Pillar says in my ears. "Not too shabby for our first day at college," he pulls his sarcasm on me. "See you in the asylum tonight," he hangs up on me.

"Are you okay?" I ask the girl as I catch my breath.

She nods. "As soon as you told me your name was Alice, I knew I was going to be okay. Thank you."

"Really?" I check her body for any bruises. "Are you hurt in any way?"

The girl shakes her head no. I can tell she is alright. The Cheshire didn't hurt her, which makes me wonder what all of this was about.

"What's your name?" I run my finger through her hair.

"Constance."

"What a lovely name," I hug her again.

"Not as lovely as yours," her small hands cling to my pullover from behind. "My mom was going to name me Alice first."

"You love that name a lot, huh?" I smile, wondering why my name means so much to her.

She hit me right with the answer, "The man who kidnapped me told me a girl named Alice was coming for me."

"Oh." My face tightens, and my need to catch the Cheshire heightens. "Did you see his face?"

"No, he was wearing a mask of a grinning cat," she said. "But when I asked him if it was Alice in Wonderland who was coming to save me, he said yes, it was her. He meant you," the girl continues, her head on my shoulder. I fight the tears not to cry. She thinks Alice is her hero from the books, and that she came to save her. Or maybe I am too stupid to notice that she is right. That I am Alice, and that I am destined for much more than a cell in an asylum. "I told him Alice is only seven," the girl continues. "She can't save me."

"What did he say to that?"

"He said, 'Alice is grown up now, and she will try to save the world.'"

Chapter 28

The Radcliffe Lunatic Asylum, Oxford

Going back to the Radcliffe Asylum, I don't know what's worse: the mad people inside, or the mad people outside.

Dr. Tom Truckle taunts me for ten minutes for being late and jeopardizing his reputation by being a hero. He doesn't care whatsoever about saving the girl. I feel better about the way the Pillar blackmails him. Also, I try to tell him to get over it. I had shoved the girl out to the public and escaped through the window Jack used. No one had seen me save her but the Pillar's chauffeur, and the few tourists who cannot prove anything but the existence of a mad girl who ate a block of cheese at the Great Hall. Then of course, the media began showing the video of the mad girl who ate the block of cheese, and began connecting me to saving the girl.

Tom permits me to see the Pillar one last time, before I am shoved back to the ward underground. He has given my Tiger Lily to the Pillar, just to anger me. Now, I will have to get it from the Pillar.

As I walk the VIP lounge, I don't think I could have done much without the Pillar whom I have no idea what to think of. And Jack, who is a total mystery. The fact that every passing second brings me closer to the idea of the existence of a real Wonderland, that everyone I meet seems to be part of it, is both enchanting and maddening at the same time.

I sit on the chair facing the Pillar's bars, feeling super powerful though.

"Some people say that Lewis Carroll must have been on drugs to write such a whimsical, nonsensical, and radical tale as Alice's Adventures Under Ground," the Pillar shoots me with one of his seemingly irrelevant remarks, like always. He doesn't even glance at me, treating the hookah as if he's fixing his new Porsche.

"In Wonderland, you mean." I fidget, caught in his mad reality again.

"It was called Under Ground, until Lewis published his first draft in 1865," the Pillar educates me. "Two thousand copies were published before he came to his senses and collected them back from the market, to republish it again as Alice's Adventures in Wonderland."

"Why did he do that?" I am astonished at the way he can change the conversation. I thought we were going to talk about what happened today.

"That's a big question," he wiggles his gloved finger. "I don't really have the answer. Historians will tell you that John Tenniel, his genius painter, wasn't satisfied with the pictures. The truth is, Lewis hid a lot of messages inside the book, which at first draft, didn't seem that hidden to Tenniel. Lewis needed to rewrite it one last time."

"Did he succeed in pulling back the two thousand copies from the market?"

"All but fifty copies," the Pillar raises his copy, as if he is holding the Olympic torch. "This is one of them."

"So that's why you treat it like your personal Wonderland bible."

"I don't think I am a bible man, Alice--I love comics though," he says "But I get your metaphor. There are chapters in here that have never been seen by human eyes." He steps to a brighter spot in the cell. For the first time, I notice that something is wrong with the Pillar's skin. It's why he probably wears too much cloth. It's like he has a mild allergy, and it looks like his skin is slightly peeling off.

"Why did the Cheshire tell Constance that a girl named Alice was going to save her?" I cut in. There are so many questions in my head. I need an answer to one or two, at least.

"Isn't it strange when you talk about Alice in third person, as if it's not you?"

I shrug. It's the question I have been escaping all day. "I am not Alice," I tell him, even though Constance made me think I must be her. But thinking it over on my way back, I found the idea unbelievable. "I can't be, not even logically. The real Alice lived in the 19th century. We're in the 21st."

"When it comes to Wonderland, what's logic got to do with it?" he says. "You know what I think? I think you're afraid to be Alice."

"Why would you say that?"

"Because you think you're fragile. The craziness you've seen in the so-called sane world is too much for you." His eyes are unusually piercing. "I mean, just click your TV on and look at the madness in the world. Wars, killing, envy, hatred, and the whole nine yards. It doesn't look too encouraging, going out there and helping people, not when you could just spend your time in this cozy cell and bed downstairs. It's easy downstairs, isn't it?" He cranes his head forward. "You're sure you got a place to sleep at night. You don't have worries about tomorrow. And in your case, you have no past to haunt you. And all you have to do in exchange for food is entertain the wardens with thirty minutes of shock therapy every now and then. Life is just so easy for the mad."

I find my hands laced together as I listen to his words. I hate how he sees right through me. I haven't thought about it like that exactly, but he hit the jackpot about the world outside. I wasn't comfortable with it, and had wished I could return to the crazy cell I was trying to escape all of the time. It's a horrible feeling. It feels inhuman and wrong. But so is my fear of the sane people out there. When I think of it, I haven't met a Mushroomer downstairs who is capable of trapping a girl in a dark crawlspace, like the Cheshire did.

"You know who mad people really are, Alice?" the Pillar speaks with his pipe between his lips. "Just lazy people who took the easier way out in life."

"Please give me some of that stuff you're smoking." I try to make it sound like a joke, hiding the fact that he is getting to me. "It seems very good."

"Beware of what you wish for, Alice," he says. "I'm one of the few Lewis wrote about accurately. I mean, without mushrooms, hookahs, and smoke, where would I be?" he stands up and starts tapping his feet in place. It's funny seeing him dance and enjoy himself. Whether he is a real killer or a hoax still puzzles me.

"May I ask why you're dancing now?"

"It's not a dance. It's a Caucus Race. You run so fast, still in the same place," he says, so into it. "It reminds me that we can't escape our fates. But enough about me, Alice. How did it feel to save Constance today?"

"It felt..." I shrug. "It felt really good. Heart-wrenching, but good. I feel like if I end up living in the sane world, I need to save a soul every day to cling to my sanity."

The Pillar smiles broadly.

"What's that smile on your face?"

"You said it yourself," the Pillar says. "The only way to stay sane in the world outside is to save a soul every day. How about we do it again? And then maybe, again?"

"I thought I was getting out to prove my sanity. Is that what I am here for? To save people from mad people and Wonderland Monsters?"

"Questions. Questions. Questions. Don't you ever learn that questions don't ever get answered unless I ask them?" he says. "Questions are the lazy man's way to try to learn, when the only way to learn is not to ask."

"Then what is the only way to learn?"

"To live, of course," he tilts his head. "Look at me. Not really a role model, but I am a fine example of living. You'd think I'm stoned and lightheaded, but you know that the stuff I learned is endless. That's because I allowed myself to live every moment of it."

"Whatever," I stand up. "I said it as a metaphor. I don't really want to save someone every day. The outside world is too mad for me," I let out an uncontrolled laugh. "I think I better stay here. I believe you promised me I'd get my Tiger Lily back." I see it next to the couch. Someone has been taking care of her. She looks fine.

"As you wish, Alice," he pushes the pot my way. "As you wish."

I take the pot, and feel its warmth in my heart. I paid a great price to get my friend back.

Chapter 29

Underground Ward, the Radcliffe Asylum, Oxford

Holding my precious pot, I walk among my fellow mad people back to my room. Waltraud taps her prod on her hand as she walks behind me. The patients on both sides stare at me, wondering where I have been all day. It's as if they secretly know I have been to the outside world, and are wondering what it was like. I smile at them and they tilt their heads, wondering why I am smiling today.

I know why. I am back home.

Waltraud informs me that it's too late for me to start shock therapy, but she promises me great pain soon. She and Ogier aren't finished with me yet, after I tried escaping last time. I see a plaster on her nose from when I pushed her face in the bucket. Whatever pain they impose on me, it won't be as bad as knowing there are killers out there killing young girls.

I enter my cell and place my flower next to the wall with the slight crack in it. Tomorrow she'll enjoy sunshine for ten minutes again. Before I lay to sleep, I run my fingers on the writing on the wall. It still says the fourteenth of January and has a key drawn underneath. I know for a fact that we're not in January. It's mid-December. Christmas is on the way. I have no idea what the date means. Why January the fourteenth?

As for the key, I have no clue what it means. Who wrote this on my wall?

Tired of questioning, I call it a day, and lay me down to sleep.

***

Usually my dreams in the asylum are short and make no sense. This time I dream of standing at a bus stop. I look younger, probably seventeen. I'm holding someone's hand. I think it must be Adam J. Dixon's. His is wearing a hood and I can't see his face. My first impression is that he is not Adam. He could be the Pillar playing games with me. Even worse, the Cheshire Cat. After all, I don't know what Adam and the Cheshire look like. How can I forget the face of someone I loved?

Whoever I am holding hands with squeezes it in a gentle way. It's a warm squeeze, filled with love and care. I need it. I haven't felt this safe before. It's not the Cheshire or the Pillar. It has to be Adam.

A number of other students come over and wait at the bus stop. They are all happy. They are laughing. They high-five Adam and talk to him. They call him *Aay Jay*. I am afraid they'll ignore me. None of their faces ring a bell, and they are supposed to be my classmates.

"Alice!" a girl cheers. And then another. They raise their hands to high-five me. Hesitantly, I clap back. They ask me how I have been. One girl whispers in my ear that she had always had an eye on Adam, but now that we're together, she wishes me luck. She doesn't say it in a mean way. She is happy for me. She even points at my sisters, Lorina and Elsie, standing at the bus stop opposite to us. They don't say a word. Their eyes say it all. They don't like me.

Adam is taller than me. He bows his head with the hood still on and whispers in my ear. "I heard that," his voice is so musical, I want to play it over and over again. "They don't know that *I* am the lucky one," he squeezes my hand again.

The bus arrives before I get to talk back to him, or see his face. He pulls me ahead and we get on the yellow bus. The atmosphere is ethereal. Everything just fits. I think the sky is even pinkish in my dream. If this was my life before the asylum, then I'm better off dead now, without Adam and my friends.

Yes, I know I'm dreaming and it seems I'm the only who knows this is in the past. The others are just happy, cracking jokes. I am supposed to have spent a lot of time with them, but I don't remember one face. The bus takes off, and I'm starting to doubt we're heading to school, or we wouldn't be that happy.

Adam keeps talking to the others, while I'm occupied with the bus. My sisters said I killed everyone on a bus. Could it be this one? I stand up and walk the aisle, looking for a stranger on the bus. It's my gut feeling that tells me there is an intruder in here. I know I'm not crazy. I couldn't have killed all those happy people I seem to love. Why would I?

I eye each passenger, but don't see someone I know or suspect. It even crosses my mind that I might find my envious sisters on the bus. Maybe they did it, but they aren't here.

I reach the beginning of the bus, near the driver's seat, when I realize who the intruder is. The bus driver has rabbit ears.

I rub my eyes and stare back at everyone. They don't seem to see it. I take a step forward and notice the sign says the bus is driving to 83 St. Aldates Street in Oxford, the same street where I got off at the Tom Tower this morning.

"You're late, you're late, for a very important date," a voice mocks me. A voice I hate the most. It's the rabbit driver. He is the same rabbit I see in the mirror, with his white hair dangling down his face, except I can see his teeth now. They are pointed, like a scary clown. The rabbit has a pocket watch dangling from his hand.

"Leave me alone," I say. "I'm not mad."

"How is this for madness?" The rabbit pushes the gas pedal and speeds up, crossing over to the opposite side of the road. The bus is swooshing against the cars driving our direction. He wants to kill us all. I jump on him and grip the wheel, trying to stop the bus, but the rabbit is too strong. I can't steer the wheel.

My friends in the back scream, "Don't do it, Alice! Don't kill us!"

I have no idea why they think it's me. I turn back and the rabbit is gone. The bus is on the loose. When I raise my head to look at the cars, glass splinters in my face. We've already crashed. It's time to wake up from the dream. How in the world did I survive this?

Chapter 30

Public Transportation Bus, Oxford

I wake up shaking in my seat. Yes, I am in a seat, and on a bus. Not the one in my dream, but a real one, outside of the asylum.

"Bad dreams?" the Pillar rests both his hands on a cane next to me. We're sitting in the front seat of the bus. I crane my head to see the driver. He isn't a rabbit. Instead, it's that mouse-looking dude who must be working for the Pillar. He is wearing an Irish hat this time.

The sun is shining feebly outside. I think it's the next day already.

"I dreamt of a school bus," I rub my eyes, checking out my modern Alice outfit. "Am I still dreaming?"

"Hit the brakes, please!" he shouts at the bus driver, who hits the breaks abruptly. Cars screech and people honk their horns behind us, as I almost bang my head on the pole.

"Does this feel like a dream to you?" the Pillar says, and signals for the driver to proceed.

"You stole a public bus?" I furrow my eyebrows.

"Rich people steal poor people's houses and lives. I can't borrow a public bus?" he shakes his shoulder, sincerely annoyed by my remark.

"How did I get here?" I mop my head. I am not hurt.

"I had to sedate you, and dress you up," the Pillar looks out of the window. "The Mushroomers helped me."

"Why would you do something like that?" I am dizzy and enraged by the Pillar dragging me out here. "I told you, I am done with the world outside. I am not the Alice you think I am."

"There is something you have to see." The Pillar knocks his cane on the floor. "Stop here!" he says, raising his cane. I notice he never addresses the chauffeur by name. "Take this," he tucks a notebook in my lap. It looks like it belongs to a child, with pink and yellow roses on the cover. It's a little smeared with ashes or something though.

"What's this?" I open it up and flip through it. The notebook is girlish. Its pages are filled with drawings of a young girl in a blue-and-white dress. At one point, the girl is fighting a Cheshire Cat, then the Mad Hatter, and the Jabberwocky. It's basically a young girl's re-imagining of a twisted Wonderland. The Alice in the drawing looks uncannily like me.

"It's Constance's notebook," the Pillar explains. "She drew all this three years ago, when she was seven years old."

"So what? The girl looks a little like me. It doesn't mean I am the Alice she wants. I look pretty ordinary, like any other girl on the street."

"That's not the point. Constance had this book with her when the Cheshire kidnapped her. Her mother called and asked for it, since it was left in the fireplace in Christ Church."

"Her mother called who?" I wonder.

"Doesn't matter. She said Constance asked for you to deliver it. The girl wants to see you one last time. That's her house." He points at a two-story middle-class house. It's mostly gray, but in a lovely way.

I stare at the house and then at the notebook. The truth is, I love Constance. I actually miss her, and it's only been a day, when I only talked to her for ten minutes.

"Alright," I sigh. "If that's all, I will deliver it."

Chapter 31

Constance's House

The doorbell to Constance's house is a cuckoo's voice. I try not to laugh at the irony.

"Just a minute," a woman's voice calls from inside. A moment later, she opens the door.

"Hi," I bend my head slightly. "My name is…"

"Alice," the woman says. She looks like Constance's grandmother, but she must be her mother. Her eyes are moistened. Was she crying? "I know." She pulls me closer, and hugs me. Actually, she is squeezing me, and her armpits smell. I expect more hygiene from sane people, but I say nothing. "We were waiting for you."

"I brought you this," I show her the notebook.

Constance's mother stares at the notebook for a while, then breaks into tears. It's the kind of sniffling tears that make you think the person is sneezing in your face. I understand she is emotional, but I am bringing her the notebook. She should be happy.

"It's Constance," she holds it in her hands. Constance is the kind of word that is pretty good for spitting. She almost drenches me.

"I know," I smile. "Can I see her? I was told…"

The mother breaks into tears again. She needs a handkerchief and I have none. Why does she keep crying? "Come in," she ushers me inside. Finally.

I walk into the modest house, but don't get to look around, since the mother pulls me by the hand to Constance's room.

Constance's room is all about Alice in Wonderland. All kinds of wallpapers, toys... even the carpet has one big Humpty Dumpty on it. In between, there is always Alice, fighting dragons, wolves, and human-sized spiders. All the Alices are me. If I had doubts about the notebook, I can't escape a wall-size portrait of me.

This isn't happening. How could it be?

"She always talks about you," her mother explains. "I've always wondered why you never showed up. She said she keeps inviting you to dinner, but you're busy saving lives."

"I..." I am speechless, afraid that I'll burst into tears when Constance comes through the door. Did the Cheshire Cat plan this on purpose?

"Yesterday, she told me that even if the Cheshire kidnaps her again, you promised her you will always save her."

"Of course...."

"And now that it's happened, I believe you're here to..."

"What's happened?" I interrupt.

Suddenly, we both realize the horror. She doesn't know why I am here, and I don't know why I am here. The Pillar played me.

"You don't know?" her mother looks puzzled. "Constance was kidnapped again yesterday by the Cheshire."

"What? How?" I slump to the bed, tears filling my eyes but refusing to burst out. "Didn't the police protect her? What is this, a jungle? The Cheshire kidnaps a girl twice? Why didn't you take care of her?"

"She wasn't taken here," her mother explains. "She went to the Alice Shop in Oxford. She was planning on buying you a present."

"The Alice Shop?"

"Yes. You must know it. It's on 83 St. Aldates."

Chapter 32

St. Aldates Street, The Alice Shop, Christ Church

It takes me some time to find the Pillar. He keeps playing that silly game with me on the phone where he sends me messages and guides me through town to find him. Instead of firing back at him for playing me, he's disarming my anger by using the tactic of wait. I have no choice but to play his game. At this moment, I have no one else but him to help me catch the Cheshire.

And I will catch him. I feel so close to Constance, and this is beginning to become personal between me and the Cheshire.

I end up in front of the Alice Shop at 83 St. Aldates Street. It's a gift shop, really nice. It screams Victorian style, but has a red door with the number 83 on it. A young crowd visits and leaves with a Queen of Hearts playing card, a drinking bottle that says 'drink me,' a big fluffy rabbit in a tuxedo, and all kinds of souvenirs.

A breeze of cold air rushes behind me all of a sudden. When I turn around, I see it's a school bus speeding up. It's just a normal bus, and nothing bad is going to happen. It just reminds me of my dream, where the rabbit killed my friends. Why does everyone else think I killed them? I don't even know what's real and what isn't.

My phone rings.

"Historians will tell you that the Alice Shop is what inspired Lewis to write about the Old Sheep Shop in Alice's Adventures Through the Looking Glass," the Pillar says on the phone. "The truth is, this is the shop itself. Lovely, isn't it?"

"Can't quite say that, after you shattered my childhood memories." I purse my lips.

"You don't have 'childhood' memories. You have Wonderland memories. They will come back to you sooner or later. I don't promise you will like them, though."

"So why did I dream about the Alice Shop?"

"I can't think of something that could help in that shop. It's just the shop the Cheshire followed Constance to. That's it. Tourists come to visit it from all over the world. Constance just loved you so much, she wanted to buy you something special from it," the Pillar says, and I don't know his location. "The fact that you dreamed about it, only backs up my theory that you're destined to save lives outside the asylum. You still want to stay lazy in your cell downstairs?"

"No," I'm confident about it. "If not to save lives, then to save Constance and catch the Cheshire this time."

"Can you write this down and sign it please, so I can use it in court when you change your mind again?" he says.

"Stop playing games. I learned my lesson. If Constance thinks I am her superhero, I will be. So don't waste time, and tell me something useful. Why did the Cheshire kidnap her again, after I saved her?"

"Maybe you didn't really save her the first time. Maybe he let you save her."

"How so?"

"Maybe he just let you think you saved her," the Pillar says. "So he could know if you're the real Alice because if so, you'll be a great threat to him."

"How can I be a threat to the Cheshire? And why don't you just tell me what happened in Wonderland in the past?"

"Other than the fact that I don't know everything, I have to protect certain assets of mine. Wonderland is like relationships, very complicated. Do I have to remind you that you and I weren't allies in Wonderland?" his voice is sharp, as if he wants to carve the recognition into my skull.

"I didn't think I was friends with a serial killer," I rebound.

The Pillar says nothing for some time. His silence is killing me. All kinds of crazy thoughts fill my head.

"I am really wondering what the Cheshire is after," like always, he is a master of changing subjects. "Killing girls for fun isn't his thing. He is smart, sneaky, sly, and smooth, just like a normal cat. A killing spree isn't his thing."

"Then where do I start looking for him? He must have a weak spot." I begin walking around the college. It feels good walking and breathing the air, like a normal person. I am starting to get used to it.

"In my caterpillar experience, a man's weakness always lies in their past, where all their dirty laundry is buried," he sighs cheeringly.

Chapter 33

"How do we dig into his past?" I glance skyward, wondering if he's watching me from somewhere. I am not sure he is back in the asylum. He sounds as if he's around me. I don't know why.

"Why don't you think for yourself for a change?" the Pillar says.

I think it over for a moment. What do I know about the Cheshire? "The Cheshire likes games. His games are meticulously planned. He is fond of making them about grins and cats, his favorite subjects. He is also fond of hinting to his past...wait. Is that it? You said that Cheshire County and the cheese factory inspired Lewis to write about him."

"It's a very small town. Lovely sane people, lazy as well. They haven't cherished Lewis Carroll's memory enough, so they stayed a small town. I wouldn't expect answers from them," the Pillar says, "I like your thinking though, Alice. But you're like most sane people, looking in a faraway place, when the answer is right under your feet." The way he says 'feet,' makes me stop in my place. Why am I so sure he is nearby? I know now. All the sounds surrounding him are the same sounds around me. The cars, the sound of the man selling waffles, the girls squeaking out of the Alice Shop.

"Literally, Alice," he demands. "Look under your feet."

I look at my white sneakers and wonder what he means. Am I supposed to see a mark on the pavement now? I wouldn't be surprised if that is the case.

Finally, something crazy happens. A book falls from the sky, right in front of me. It's Alice's Adventures Under Ground.

Without glancing skyward again, I kneel down and pick it up, making sure the copy is intact. Then I crane my head up. The Pillar is standing at the roof of Tom Quad, one of the four quadrangles in Christ Church. He is standing in a spot right next to the Tom Tower. I prefer not to ask how he got there. "That's not a gentle way to treat a book that was never out in print," I tell him on the phone, and wave 'hi' to him with the book.

He pretends he doesn't know me and feeds pigeons from his gloved hands. "Did you know that the Lewis family doesn't make a dime out of its sales?" he ignores me, but talks to me on the phone. Neat. "Can you believe that? It's the second most sold book in history, after the bible." I didn't know that. "I guess Lewis couldn't compete with God, although they are both big on nonsense." The pigeons flutter away from the roof, and I stand up with the book in my hands. No one around me even questions a book that has fallen from the sky. Only a couple of girls shoot me irritated glances and keep on walking. I have no idea why they did that. Are people that busy in the sane world?

I flip through the book like crazy. "So what page should I be reading to learn about the Cheshire's past," I jam the phone between my cheek and shoulder. "Is it the part when I talk to him about the grin?"

"You said 'I' when you mentioned talking to the Cheshire. That's progress to me," he points out. "There is only one person who might know about the Cheshire's past. She was mentioned in the book. You just need to free your mind, and the rest will follow," he whistles to the flying pigeons to come back. "Think of the first time you met the Cheshire in the book, Alice. Think."

"He was on the tree, and I was lost," I say confidently. "He kept appearing and disappearing again."

"It's a great metaphor for your current situation, but no, that's not when you first met the Cheshire. You met the Cheshire at..."

"The Duchess's house," the words spring out of my chest. "The Duchess!"

"Yes. In fact, the Duchess owned the Cheshire Cat at this point."

"I get it. If we find the Duchess, who better than her knows about the Cheshire's past, and hopefully his weaknesses." I crane my head up and look at him. "Do you know how we can find her?"

Instead of looking back at me, the Pillar raises his cane in one hand, the hookah in the other. He stares down at the pedestrians on St. Aldates Street, and then shouts at the world from the top of his lungs, "God has ordered me to build an Ark and get you on it, people!" He is acting dead serious. "If you don't get on it with me before the Wonderland Monsters arrive, you will all die. This will be your apocalypse!"

I try not to laugh, while a couple of homeless people faintly clap their hands next to me. "Yeah, the apocalypse. I remember it," a toothless man says, then goes asking someone for change. Other than this, no one even pays attention at the Moses-posing man on the roof.

The Pillar lowers his instruments and looks down at me with that smug grin on his face. "Don't you love the carelessness of the sane world? I mean, I could be wrapped up in dynamite and no amount of warning will make them do something about it," his whole face is shimmering with delight. Then in a blink of an eye, he changes to dead serious again. "Are you ready to meet the Duchess?"

Chapter 34

"I don't suppose she is really a 'Duchess' in this time and age," I stop next to the Pillar, watching the news on a TV that's for sale behind a shopping window. He came down from the rooftop and we started walking, but something about the TV caught his attention.

"Of course not," the Pillar says absently, glancing at another TV next to it. It's broadcasting news about people being evacuated from their homes. "I told you the Wonderland Monsters were reincarnated into modern day people. The Duchess is reincarnated into what you'd call the equivalent of a 'Duchess' in our time." He is still taken by the news. There's a documentary about poverty in African countries. I don't know what's so interesting to him, and I can't read his face.

"Equivalent? What is she?" I ponder. "Wait. The Duchess isn't the Queen of England, is she?"

"Oh, no," the Pillar finally looks away from the horrible news all over the world. "That's just silly," he tells me.

"As if all the rest isn't."

"Silly is different from nonsense. Queens of England have always been fond of Lewis. As a matter of fact, Queen Victoria was a good friend of his."

"Then who is the Duchess?"

"Margaret Kent," the Pillar announces.

"Who?"

"A very well-known woman in the Parliament," he says.

"The British Parliament?"

"No. The Parliament of Oz. Focus, Alice," the Pillar pouts. "She is a TV superstar," he points at another TV behind the glass window, showing a meeting of the British Parliament. There are too many important people in suits. I don't know who Margaret Kent is. "I don't expect you to recognize her. You've been living underground for years. But she is loved by most sane people."

"How is the Duchess loved by other people? Isn't she supposed to be a Wonderland Monster?"

"Like most politicians, she's fooled them by promising the impossible," the Pillar says. "Did you ever notice if you promised the possible, people won't believe you?"

"She is one of those people with two different faces. How wasn't she exposed until now?"

"Some have tried, actually. A year ago, a young man drew a caricature of her in the Daily Telegraph, mocking her as the ugliest woman in Britain."

"Is she that ugly?" I scan all the women of the Parliament on the screen. They all look just fine.

"In fact, she is modestly beautiful, with all her plastic surgeries, pearl necklaces, and elegant blonde hair," the Pillar says. "Her ugliness mentioned in the newspaper stems from all the ugly things she does under the table. Bribes, extortion, and tampering with trials in favor of the big guys. One of the rules of the sane world… the poor keep getting poorer, and the rich keep getting…bitcher."

"Margret Kent?" I try the name on my lips, as I recognize her from the plate in front of her as she speaks on TV. She looks like the perfect female politician, a face everyone would normally trust.

"Of course, the artist who drew the caricature was mysteriously assassinated by a 'terrorist' a week later."

"That's awful."

"Alice," the Pillar holds me by the shoulder. "You're not focusing. The artist was assassinated by someone sent by Margaret Kent because he was exposing her dirty laundry."

"Are you sure?"

"And do you know who assassinated him?" the Pillar's face is too close to mine. I have an idea about the answer, but it just refuses to surface on my lips. "The Cheshire Cat was the Duchess's grinning cat in the book. In real life, he is her private assassin."

I take a step back, my hands on the wall. My head is dizzy, and I get that feeling again, that the world in my private cell is a better place than all of this. "This can't be," my voice is almost inaudible as it starts to rain all of a sudden.

Chapter 35

"This is how the world operates," the Pillar says. We're sitting in the back of his limousine. "Why do you think killers like me and the Cheshire don't get caught? People like Margaret Kent are occupied with making money and getting more powerful every day. There is famine, wars, people dying, and poverty all around us. But you know what? The heck with all that. Let's just make more money, and kill anyone who gets in the way. Or better, let's drive them insane."

"So Margaret Kent knows about Wonderland, and hires its monsters to do her dirty work?"

"Genius, isn't it?" the Pillar says, the pipe tucked in the corner of his mouth. "You get to hire someone like the Cheshire who in the public eye is just a silly cat in a book, and then get away with it. If someone tries to expose you, he will be laughed at because, let's face it, Wonderland can't be real."

"Why is the Cheshire Cat doing it? You said it wasn't like him to go on a killing spree."

"Even a cat has to make a living," the Pillar says. "The money is good, and he has some kind of a grudge against humanity. Maybe someone stepped on his tail or something. Who knows?"

"So Margaret Kent paid him to kill the girls?"

"It's unlikely. Who'd pay to kill young girls? Besides, he wouldn't be playing games and puzzles with us, if he were being paid. Margaret's jobs are swift. She wants to get off with her enemies' heads."

"So how are we going to make Mrs. Kent tell us anything about the Cheshire?" I say. "Is it even possible we could meet such an important woman in the first place?"

The Pillar turns to me with that shimmering look in his eyes again. "It depends."

"On?"

"Tell me, Alice," he rubs something off his trousers. "On a scale from one to insanity, how insane are you?"

I get the feeling that the Pillar and I are about to do some crazy things.

Chapter 36

"I'm not going to do that!" Tom Truckle protests. He fidgets in his place, and reaches for his pills from the drawer.

The Pillar and I sit opposite to him in his office. We exchange looks, while we're on the verge of bursting into laughter. I have to admit that spending time with the Pillar has taught me to just let go and give in to all the madness in the world.

"I am not asking much," I tell Truckle. "I just want a Certificate of Insanity."

"There is no such thing," Truckle gulps water to let the pill slide down. "And even if there is, I just can't do it. This is insane. *You* are insane."

"See, that's why I want a Certificate of Insanity," I am doing my best not to giggle.

"Please, Tommy," the Pillar rests his hands on his cane. "We've got work to do, and you're stalling."

"You are insane as well," Truckle says.

"Thank you, but I don't need a certificate myself. It's poor Alice here who needs it," the Pillar sulks. "Look at her. She is so innocent." I pull my legs together and squeeze my hands between them, flapping my eyelashes and sulking all over him. I'm really enjoying this. "How else can we prove she is insane?" the Pillar adds.

"Something tells me you're going to do something mad with this certificate." Truckle is losing it. The pressure the Pillar is putting him under is unbelievable. The doctor is breaking all the rules to keep his job.

"Please don't use words like 'mad' and 'retarded.' It's really hurts." The Pillar is playing this just right. I am going to laugh until I cry when I get out.

"I didn't say 'retarded!'" Truckle grips his chair, face red like a tomato before explosion. "Besides, what do you want me to call you?"

"Mushroom is a good word. Right, Alice?" the Pillar looks at me.

"Yes," I blink my eyes innocently again. "Mushroom. I am a Mushroom." The Pillar nods and pats me gently. "You're a Mushroom," I address the Pillar, then turn to Dr. Truckle. "And you're a Mushroom, too."

"I'm not a Mushroom!" Dr. Truckle stands up, slamming his hands on the desk. I think he should seriously consider reporting the Pillar's escape and lose his job, or he'll end up in one of the underground wards.

"Yes you are," I push it, then stare at him as if he is sick. "You have those red spots on your face. What are those, Dr. Truckle?"

"What?" He touches his face. "What spots?"

"I think it may be chickenpox," the Pillar worsens the joke. "*Mushroompox*, maybe?"

"You're messing with my head!" Dr. Truckle screams. I can see the veins pumping on his neck. "Here is your certificate," he pulls out an official paper from the drawer and signs it. "Get out!"

The Pillar cranes his head to see what Dr. Truckle is writing. "Please, Dr. Truckle. Don't write that," he protests.

Dr. Truckle looks puzzled.

"What did he write?" I stand up and stomp my feet. "Is it about me?" I fold my arms in front of me.

"He wrote," the Pillar pretends he can't bring himself to say it. "He wrote that you're 'insane in the membrane,' and 'cuckoo in the head.'"

"Did you write that?" I sneer at Dr. Truckle.

"No." Dr. Truckle waves his defensive arms. "I swear, I didn't."

I pull the certificate angrily, then read it. It's what we're looking for. The Pillar and I stand up, ready to leave. But before we go, I get on the desk and kiss Dr. Truckle on the cheek, then run my hands slowly upon his nose. We've played the poor guy too much. When I kiss him, it's like I've electrocuted him with my lips. I think he is going to pee himself. "And you haven't even tried shock therapy yet," I whisper in his ear.

"Let's go, Alice," the Pillar says. "We're late for our plane to London." He waves my Certificate of Insanity in front of him. We're going to need it to meet the Duchess.

Chapter 37

Margaret Kent's Office, the Westminster Palace, London

Margaret Kent sat alone in a private luxurious room in the Palace of Westminster in London. She had an important meeting to attend in a little while, and she didn't like waiting. If she'd ever waited for anyone, she wouldn't have come this far in her career. Things had to be done swiftly, and decisions had to be made in a flash of an eye. In order to save a few heads, many heads had to be chopped. She learned that from the Queen of Hearts many years ago. But she didn't want to remember Wonderland anymore. She had moved on, and now she had to deal with things in this world.

Ordinary people would think that a woman of her caliber would have everything at the tip of her fingers. It was far from it. Since Margaret joined the Parliament, she'd been having a hard time sleeping at night. The horrible things she had permitted behind the public's back were enough to drive her mad for the rest of her life.

But these horrible things had to be done she thought, as she rubbed her expensive Rolex around her wrist. A woman in such a position had to sacrifice others in favor of her nation. It was the way things were done. In the states. In Germany. And in most countries. She stood up and gazed out her window at all the simple people enjoying life outside. If they only knew the price she, and her fellow men and women of the Parliament paid to get them there.

But that's a lie, Margaret. Her annoying inner voice spoke. Not everything you have done was for the safety of your people, or everyone would have lived a generous life in this world by now.

Margaret walked away from the window and checked her hair in the mirror. In reality, it was thinning. But thanks to her personal crew who took care of her appearance, it looked far from it. People loved their politicians to look good. Beauty was a must when telling lies.

She gazed at her watch one more time, trying to distract herself from her nagging inner thoughts.

Welcome back, Margaret. It's me, the true voice inside you. The one that knows all your secrets. I know about the people you wrongfully imprisoned, sent to asylums, and even killed. It's understandable. It's a game called life.

Margaret didn't know why her annoying voice was attacking her today. She'd never regretted anything she'd done. The secrets she kept from the public were a necessary evil. If anyone thought it was possible to spread justice and make everyone equal in this world, they were highly delusional. The world was like clockwork. In order for the bigger wheels to survive, the smaller wheels had to work harder in their merry go round. They just had to be promised big things that weren't going to happen. Problem solved.

Turning her TV on to distract herself, she realized what worried her. It was right in front of her; the Cheshire Cat killing girls all around the country, while they couldn't do anything about it. They were going to discuss that in their private meeting. It had to be in private, because they all knew what the Cheshire did for them, and the secrets he knew. He'd been pushing the envelope, while they couldn't catch him because he had the power to expose them.

Margaret had been using the Cheshire for some time. She'd never known him to be a crazy killer, spilling blood for no reason. He hated humans and did the jobs she'd assigned him in exchange for money or information, mostly involving Wonderland. The Cheshire was obsessed with opening the secret doors to Wonderland again. The ones Lewis Carroll had locked the monsters in a long time ago. Margaret never knew how the Cheshire escaped his prison, and she never asked.

Ironically, her peers in the office still loved to call her "the Duchess," because as much as she faked her beautiful appearance, the ugliness inside her was always coming through. She never hesitated hurting anyone. Her career was her reason to live, and she was getting greedier every day.

"Now what am I going to do about that?" she talked to herself in the empty room. The Cheshire had to stop his killing, or the consequences were going to be grand.

Margaret Kent, fiddling with her pearl necklace, squinted at the sight of the girl she saw on TV. It was that girl who had been famous for nibbling like crazy on a block of cheese inside the Great Hall. Some said she saved the girl who'd been kidnapped by the Cheshire yesterday. The news said she was an Oxford University freshman. Still, no one could find her since.

Margaret squinted harder and neared the TV. "Wait a minute," her eyes widened, taking a closer look at the girl. "This couldn't be. Is this her?"

Chapter 38

*Entrance, the Westminster Palace, the British Parliament
headquarters*

The Pillar is pushing me in a wheelchair. We're heading
toward the Palace of Westminster's entrance. This is going to
be crazy.

I am wearing my tattered nightgown from the asylum, and
am tucked in the wheelchair. I have my legs crossed
awkwardly, and I wear one sock with a hole in it. My other
foot is dirty with mud, and my hand is hanging loose to my
side. To add some drama to the madness, I raise my other
hand in the air, as if I am a marionette left hanging by a
thread. My hair looks as if it was fried and dried, sticking
out like spikes everywhere. It's topped with a flower-colored
hat, the kind you put on toddlers.

The hat's laces are knitted like shoelaces around my neck,
but that's not the best part. White liquid is drizzling from
my mouth. People think it's vomit, but it's actually
marshmallows. I stuff my mouth with them discreetly, chew
them until they are mushy enough, and then let them drizzle
out from between my lips. It was the Pillar's idea.

I am doing my best not to laugh again, acting like a total
loon, as the Pillar wheels me across the Parliament's
entrance. The guards stop him. They speak politely, since I
look pathetic and he looks like a homeless dad on a pension
he's never collected.

"Good morning, government!" the Pillar salutes them. He is wearing blue overalls with nothing underneath, and big torn shoes. His peeling skin shows on his shoulder, and makes him look even worse. The tattered parts of his overalls are sewn with pieces of cloth. One of them is the badge of the Liverpool football team, the other is the flag of the United Kingdom, with the Queen smoking a hookah on it.

"Sir, you can't walk past this line," the guards are extremely considerate. The people around us aren't. Those in expensive suits are trying to get away from us as quickly as possible. People driving by are just laughing at us mad people.

The Pillar flashes out my Insanity Certificate, as if it's a map to Treasure Island. With the bandana on his head and the silver tooth, it suits him well. "This is a certificate from the Radcliffe Lunatic Asylum stating that my daughter is insane," the Pillar says. "She is cuckoo in the head. Loony in the toony. Nana Banana," he begins to cry. "She is all I got." When he cries, my wheelchair shakes. He is that intense. I can't stop myself from laughing, so I drool more marshmallows to hide it. Sweet marshmallows.

"Sir," the guard repeats. "We're very sorry about your daughter. But you have to leave. This is a government building."

"I know what it is," the Pillar snaps, and flashes another paper that means nothing, probably some doctor's prescription. "This is permission to meet Margaret Kent."

"What?" the guard looks puzzled.

"My daughter is dying. She has Jub Jub disease. It's a contagious infection that comes from tropical birds," the Pillar flaps his elbows like a bird's wings.

The guards back away from me. I push the limits and reach for them, like a desperate beggar. "Pleath!" I plead. A woman nearby starts to sob out of pity. I am getting cramps in my stomach, from the laughs I am holding back.

"All my daughter wants before she dies is to meet Margaret Kent," the Pillar says. "This document here is permission to meet her," the Pillar exaggerates, and shows the document sideways to everyone.

Nobody cares about checking its authenticity, but the guard. When he does, I wheel myself closer to him. "Pleath, Mithter," I reach out my marionette hands again, and cough marshmallows on his legs. The guard backs off and starts to dispatch someone inside the building.

"Didn't you see us on TV?" the Pillar says. "Margaret Kent promised to see my daughter. I know Margaret Kent is a good woman. She would never let us down, right?" the Pillar is talking to the sympathizing crowd. They nod agreeably. Pity does wonders.

A daughter of one of the observing women is licking an ice cream. I turn the wheel and stretch out my hand. "Aith Kreem!"

"I'm sorry, Madame," the Pillar says. "My daughter hasn't seen a cone this big before. You mind giving it to her?"

The woman kindly asks her daughter to give me the cone. The Pillar snatches it from her, and gives it to me as we turn to face the guards. Actually, he splashes it onto my cheeks so I look totally miserable now.

The men and women in suits start complaining about not being able to enter the building because I am blocking it. "She's got Jub Jub disease!" they yell at the guards. "And we have an important meeting we need to attend."

"I heard Jub Jub disease is lethal," a man in a suit and tie declares.

"Pleath Mithter," I roll toward the man. "I want to kith the Ducheth." I spit out marshmallows and cherry ice cream.

A senior guard appears from inside and orders the guards to let us in. "We're not going to waste all day on this," he yells at them. "Let them in."

"Thank you." I reach for him. The man jumps back away from me.

The Pillar cries tears of happiness that we're going to see Margaret Kent, and rolls me inside. I have to admit, insanity is so much fun.

Chapter 39

Westminster Palace

Inside, the receptionist tries to contact Margaret Kent to confirm our meeting, but my continued vomiting of marshmallows forces them to give us space. The Pillar shows them our fake IDs and they let us into the nearest bathroom, which we detour from, of course.

The Pillar wheels me into the nearest elevator, and tells me he knows exactly where to find the Duchess. He pulls out a hookah hose he had hidden inside the wheelchair and flashes a smile like a four year old. I grimace when I see him pull small parts from the actual hookah inside my wheelchair, too. He starts connecting them together, like Legos.

"Killers usually put together a gun silencer in this part of the movie," I mock him, wondering why we're so compatible when it comes to lunacy.

"They don't call me 'Pilla da Killa' for nothing, Alice," he says, fitting the last part in. "I advise you to suspend disbelief, because everything you'll see right now is going to be beyond crazy." My eyes watch the elevator's counter rising up, until the elevator finally stops. "Smile," the Pillar says. "It's Showtime." He wheels me into the corridors against all kinds of guards, who've been dispatched about us breaching in. A guard points his gun at us, but the Pillar whips him with his hose, blood spattering on the wall. Things start to get messy.

"You didn't have to hurt him," I protest.

"Put your morals in your back pocket please, and get them out later," he puffs smoke from his hookah, and then breathes it back into the hall in great amounts. The smoke spreads all over the corridors. "I have a job to do," he pants.

People start coughing at first, some already fainting because of his wondrous smoke. A little later, after killing a couple of guards on the way, the rest start laughing hysterically. Instead of attacking us, they can't stop laughing 'til their stomachs hurt.

"Is that laughing gas?" I say.

The Pillar doesn't answer me and high-fives a happy guard instead, right before he kicks him to the ground.

"Why am I not affected by the smoke?" I ask. I feel like a spoiled kid rolled into a crazy funhouse.

"It's the marshmallows I fed you, babydoll," the Pillar kicks Margaret's door open and wheels me in. "It's an antidote."

I am not sure how to feel about being wheeled around by a killer. Am I really doing this to save a girl, or am I just a mad girl giving myself all the excuses in the world? The Pillar doesn't kill anyone with his surreal weapons. He wounds and sedates them on our way to Margaret. I do believe the Cheshire now, saying this Wonderland War is larger than anyone thinks. I don't even know what the war is about. All my thoughts are messed up again.

The Pillar doesn't stop puffing, or hitting guards with his hose. I am wheeling myself next to him by now.

"Can we just not hurt everyone we meet?" I plead, as I pant, wheeling the chair--I am so caught up in the moment, I forget I can walk and leave the chair behind.

"The real Alice wouldn't say that," the ruthless Pillar says, hitting numbers on a pad near a golden double door. "You think those are innocent people?" The door opens, and he wheels me in.

Chapter 40
Margaret Kent's office, Westminster Palace

Pillar the Killer closes the door behind us and locks it by hitting certain code numbers on the digital pad on the inside wall. He turns around and stares at the woman sitting behind her luxurious desk. She is clinging to the sides of her chair. I can see a great view of the River Thames through the glass behind her. Once she recognizes the Pillar, she is sweating, the way I did when I was in shock therapy.

"Long time no see, Duchess," the Pillar spreads his hands. Something suddenly smells. It's his armpits. He sniffs them, and he blushes slightly when looking at me. "I guess I overplayed my part."

"Listen, Carter," the Duchess says in a challenging voice. I don't like her, but she doesn't look like a weak woman. If only the Pillar hadn't taken her by surprise. "Whatever you want, I can give you."

"Did I say you can talk?" the Pillar races up to her and grabs her by the neck. Again, for a short man, his agility is superhuman. "This isn't the Parliament of the United Kingdom anymore. It's the Pillar's one man Parliament. Welcome to my surreal democracy." He feeds her marshmallows and forces her to swallow them so she'll stay immune to his smoke for a while. Then he pulls the hose and wraps it around her neck, almost choking her, as he fixes the hookah somehow on the desk. The hose is wickedly long. He pulls it far enough and sits on a chair facing her. Then he notices a rocking chair nearby and prefers to sit on it. All this time, the Duchess is choking on the hose snaking around her neck.

"We have three minutes before the guards unlock the code on your door," the Pillar tells her. "So here is the deal. I will ask you questions. You will answer them. And I'll go away." The Duchess nods, hanging onto the hose in case he pulls harder. "If you lie to me, I will choke you to death, Margaret. It's an easy question. Where can I find the Cheshire?"

"I…" the Duchess's eyes beg for slack around her neck. The Pillar loosens his hose a little. "I truly don't know."

"I never trust anyone who says 'truly,' 'believe me,' or 'deeply.'" The Pillar doesn't pull, but he takes a drag from his hookah. It still has some pressure on the Duchess's neck.

"Believe me, I don't," she reaches out her arm. "Is that Alice?" she points at me.

"No," the Pillar says. "That's an insane underage girl with acne, angst, and parental issues. I am eloping with her. Now, answer the question. When was the last time you saw the Cheshire?"

"You know this is an absurd question," she says, her eyes glancing at me. The Pillar pulls on the hose, and she diverts her gaze to him. There is something they both don't want me to know about the Cheshire. I wonder what it is. "The Cheshire is a master of disguise."

"He is not a master of anything," I sense envy in the Pillar's voice.

"He wasn't walking around in a grinning cat's mask, for God's sake," the Duchess grunts against the hose. "I've never even seen his face since he's transformed from a cat to a human."

"But you know him when you see him," Pillar says. "Can you tell me why he is killing those girls? What's gotten into him?"

"I'd like to know that myself. Believe me, I would. All I know is that he reappeared two years ago and approached me. It was the first time I saw him since Carroll trapped the monsters in Wonderland. So I thought he'd make a good assassin. I send him the missions by email, pay with wire transfers. That's all."

"See?" the Pillar turns to me. "The government people fund assassins from Wonderland. Even Lewis Carroll couldn't have thought of that." He pulls the hose harder, looking back at the Duchess.

I am speechless. The world outside is a mess. I remind myself that the Pillar told me that from now on, I need to suspend disbelief. It's funny I have to do this in a sane world. Did the Duchess just say that Lewis Carroll locked the Wonderland Monsters away?

The Pillar takes a long drag. The Duchess's face begins to turn blue.

"Wait," she raises her hand. "I remember one last thing. I thought it was trivial, but it rings a bell now," the Duchess says.

"I am listening."

"Three months ago, the Cheshire emailed me, asking for some of Lewis Carroll's vintage photos," she says. I remind myself Lewis was a photographer. "Photos of girls, specifically."

"More than fifty percent of Lewis's photos were girls," the Pillar says. I didn't know that. "Young girls, to be precise." Now, that sounds a bit weird to me.

"I know, but the Cheshire had a list of names. Seven girls," the Duchess says. "You know that Lewis's work has never been collected properly in one volume, so the Cheshire asked me to use my connections and get him the photos."

"And you didn't think that might have anything to do with the killing spree he is on?" I feel the need to interfere.

"Sane folks, babydoll," the Pillar barely tilts his head toward me. "They love to look away from reason. It's a common symptom." He turns back to the Duchess. "What happened after you got him the photos?"

"He disappeared. A week later, the killings started," the Duchess said. "The reason why I dismissed this incident is that the names of the dead girls didn't match the girl in the photos."

"Of course they don't match," I say. "The girls Lewis photographed lived a hundred and fifty years ago. They are dead."

"Still, there has to be a connection," the Pillar contemplates. "How many girls has he kidnapped so far?"

"Six killed. Constance is the seventh," I say. Poor Constance. I'm sitting here with these mad Wonderlanders, unable to help her.

"It means if we don't save Constance, we might never find him again. I assume she is the last on the list," the Pillar says, then asks the Duchess for the list of names. She writes them down, still tilting her neck awkwardly, then asks him to let her live. "This isn't enough, Duchess. It's all too vague," the Pillar says. "Give me something better than this. A lead I can follow once I leave this office."

"I have a lead," she says, her eyes show her reluctance to speak. "I know someone who knows about the Cheshire's origins. But I doubt she will want to talk to you."

The Pillar grimaces. I assume he never had a problem forcing people to talk. "Who'd that person be? And it's a 'she?'"

"It's the White Queen."

Chapter 41

"Who is the White Queen?" I ask the Pillar, but he ignores me. I can sense he's uncomfortable talking about her. There is an undecipherable look in his eyes. All I can interpret is that he highly respects her.

"The White Queen. The chess Queen. The one in Through the Looking Glass," the Duchess replies on his behalf. She seems angry with me.

"Why would the White Queen know about the Cheshire's origins?" the Pillar asks.

"At some point in Wonderland, he confessed certain things to her. You know how charming she can be when you're down and out." The Duchess definitely hates the White Queen, too.

I watch the Pillar think about the White Queen a breath too long. It's as if he is staring into a memory. A memory so relaxing, he loosens his grip on the hose. Who is the White Queen? I'm so eager to know.

The digital pad on the wall starts to buzz, and the timer counts down.

"We have no time," the Pillar says. "The guards are on their way and I'm not into spilling sane people's blood today," he approaches the Duchess. "I'll let you go. But if I learn that you lied to me, I'm going to make you as ugly as you were in Wonderland."

"I am telling the truth. Believe me," she pleads. I can't help but wonder what the Duchess has done to become pretty if she had been ugly in Wonderland.

"One more thing before I go," the Pillar says. "I have a brother. No need for names. Just look him up. He's been to Afghanistan. He lost his arm. Came back and lost his wife, his kids, his dog, his house, and his job. Thanks to the likes of you, he is a drug addict now."

"I'm truly sorry," the Duchess lays a hand on her heart.

"I told you not to use the word, 'truly,'" he grabs her by her neck. "I want you to help him."

"Alright, alright. That's doable," she says. "We'll get him a job, extra money, insurance, and a big screen TV. We can get him a young Russian wife if you like. Anything."

I wonder how many lives the Duchess has messed with. Who does she think she is?

"I'm thinking something more elegant. He's my only brother and I love him." The Pillar rubs his chin. The word 'love' coming out of his mouth makes me cringe. "I want him to be a Tennis player. In fact, the greatest tennis player in the world. Make him win Wimbledon next year."

"I'm not God. I can't do that," she protests. "He's lost his arm for God's sake."

"It's about time a one-armed man wins something," the Pillar says. "You're the government. You promise people you can do anything."

Chapter 42

We escape the Duchess's room through a secret emergency door that leads to underground tunnels. It seems the Parliament has prepared for an apocalypse beforehand. The Duchess let the Pillar punch her in the face so she could pretend we'd attacked her before she could even see what we looked like.

The Pillar's limousine, driven by that short dude who looks like a rat picks us up around the corner. The Pillar shoves me inside and asks me not to ask any questions until we leave London. I'm tired and lay my head to rest for a while.

About two hours later, we reach Oxford. The chauffeur informs the Pillar that we're being followed.

"Who is following us?" I turn to look behind us.

"The Reds," the chauffeur says.

"Who are the Reds?" I demand an answer.

"No time for questions," the Pillar says. "Stop the car!" Again, he doesn't call his chauffeur by name.

The limousine stops, and the Pillar drags me out while we're still dressed as mad and homeless people.

"Hurry, Alice. We really have no time for the Reds right now." The Pillar walks me to the nearest bus station, and we hop on the first public transportation we come to.

"I want to know who the Reds are," I tell him once we're on, squeezed between the crowd.

"Please, stop asking." The Pillar hangs onto the pole as the bus jostles away.

"Tell me or I will tell everyone that you're a serial killer who just escaped from an asylum," I fire back, not giving two cents about the people around us. "This is crazy. I can't believe that I am still here with you."

"It's love, darling," a seated woman tells me as she examines her hair in a hand mirror.

"I think it's my mojo," the Pillar flirts with her.

"Shut up!" I block my ears from all this nonsense.

"Is this old creep hitting on you?" a boy missing a front tooth asks me. Of course, in my outfit of insanity, I must be his Princess Charming.

"Yes, I am *bugging* her," the Pillar answers him flatly. "I know teeth don't seem to be precious to you, but if you don't want to lose another one, I'd advise you to jump out of the window and die."

The boy vanishes in the blink of an eye. I don't think he realizes he was talking to Pillar the killer.

"Die, remember?" the Pillar reminds him, then faces me. "Now, can we be reasonable for a moment?"

"Reasonable?" I feel like pulling my hair out. "You call this reasonable? Ever since I met you, everything is insane!"

"I told you it's love, darling," the seated woman puts on her lipstick without looking at us.

"We met in an asylum," the Pillar winks at the woman and points at me. "Isn't it romantic?" The woman feels uncomfortable when she hears this and sits a couple of seats away. "If I remember well, all you cared about this morning was saving the little girl," the Pillar continues.

"It's still all I care about," I agree.

"So forget about the Reds and let's keep on moving," the Pillar says. "We know the White Queen can lead us to the Cheshire now. We should be going. On the way, we could look up the names of the girls the Cheshire asked for and hopefully find a connection."

"You're right," I hang onto the pole and breathe slower. I can deal with the nonsense later, after I save Constance for the second time. "So where is the White Queen? What is she in this world, a ghost in a white dress?"

"Believe me; you will never guess who she is."

"Another Wonderland Monster, I assume."

"Not at all," the Pillar smiles, as if remembering a loved one. "She is quite a nice woman. Let's not waste time, we need to get to the asylum and change before we visit her." He turns around to talk to the driver. It's not the chauffeur this time. Just a normal guy. "Bus driver, could you please let us off at the Radcliffe Lunatic Asylum?"

"It's not on my route," the driver blurts.

"I'm sure you will make an exception for two fugitive insane patients like us," the smug look on the Pillar's face is priceless. People start to part away from us now, begging the driver to send us home to the asylum.

"Thank you very much," the Pillar says and turns to me. "This way, we'll be on time to catch the plane."

"We're flying? To where?"

"The Vatican, of course."

Chapter 43

Emirate Airlines - Somewhere in the Italian Skies

It's only hours before we're on a plane to the Vatican. I don't even know what's going on. Everything is happening so fast. I feel like Alice whisked to a surreal, but real-life Wonderland.

All I am hoping is that I can save Constance in the end. At least this would be the only sane thing that happened in the last couple of days. Whenever I remember her hugging me and making me promise her I would never give up on her, I remind myself that this is why I am following the Pillar. I wonder if she's still alive.

The Pillar is looking forward to the sunset, and hoping we'll catch it while on the plane. We have a few hours before I have to be reassigned back into the asylum, as per our unbelievable deal with Dr. Truckle.

"I can't believe you blackmailed Dr. Truckle to buy us the airplane tickets," I comment, looking over the Pillar's shoulder to see the world from above. He'd insisted on sitting next to the window. Sometimes, he sounds like a four year old.

"I can't believe he didn't get us First Class tickets," the Pillar pouts. "Besides, I have never been comfortable with Emirates Airlines. I don't like their slogan: *When was the last time you did something for the first time.*"

"Why? I think it's a brilliant slogan."

"'When was the last time you did something mad.' That's a slogan, Alice."

I ignore his comment and start surfing the internet on my phone, looking up the girls' names.

"Someone's learning fast. Yesterday you weren't comfortable with typing on the phone," the Pillar notices, turns his head, and puts on his glasses. "What are you surfing? Celebrity gossip, Barbie games, and music videos?"

I discard his silliness. "Actually, I am studying the names of the girls the Cheshire killed," I say, scrolling on.

"Why the ones he killed, and not the names on the list?"

"The ones on the list are just young girls Lewis Carroll photographed," I say. "They are black and white photos, and sometimes sepia. Some of them are actually a bit creepy. I don't know what to do with those photos of girls who died a long time ago. So I had to start somewhere. The names of the Cheshire's victims seem convenient to me."

"And what did you find, Inspector Alice Wonder?" he lowers his glasses and peeks into my phone. It's one of the rare moments he looks like a real college professor.

"I researched the names of the six girls he killed," I explain. "Two of them were from the same town, and the other two from another. Only the last two were from two different towns."

The Pillar looks puzzled.

"The four towns the girls originally came from are nearby Warrington, Cheshire, where Lewis Carroll was born," I elaborate.

The Pillar raises an eyebrow. "Interesting. Anything common among the girls?"

"Not in a physical way. Not even their ages or their hobbies. Some of them were blonde, some brunettes. Some seven and some fourteen."

"But?" he cups a hand behind his ears.

"The towns they came from have something in common." I am proud of my research.

"The Towns? Curiouser and curiouser." The Pillar gives me his full attention.

"Each town the girls came from was at some point considered the origin of where Lewis Carroll was inspired to write about the Cheshire Cat."

"You didn't get that from Wikipedia, did you?" the Pillar closes his eyes and sighs.

"What's wrong with that?"

"Wikipedia to me is what Wonderland is to the so-called sane people." He opens his eyes and rubs them. "It's doesn't exist. Most of its info is Jub Jub." I am taking it that Jub Jub is the total opposite of Frabjous. "Anyways, go on. What do you think this means?"

"At first, I had no idea. I just thought their proximity to each other was a bit strange, but then I figured it out," I say. "Each of these towns has stone carvings of a grinning cat in one of its Churches."

"Grinning Cats? Churches? Never thought those two would mix," the Pillar is even more interested. "What are the names of the towns and the churches?"

"Saint Wilfrid Church in Grappenhall, a village adjacent to Lewis Carroll's birthplace in Daresbury in Warrington, Cheshire," I scroll down on my phone. "Saint Nicolas Church in Carnleigh. It's a town close to Guildford where one of Carroll's sisters lived. It also where he died. A nameless church in the village of Crof-On-Tees. And finally, St. Christopher's in Pott Shrigly."

"Each one of those churches has a statue of a grinning cat in it?"

"Each one," I nod. "And each one claims it was the inspiration for Lewis to write about the Cheshire Cat."

"That's one hell of a connection, although I can't see what it leads to," he says. "But the corpses of the Cheshire's victims were found in Cambridge, London, and Oxford."

"It's where the girls' families moved later. But the five girls were *born* in the smaller towns with the churches. Can't you see that all of these towns were visited by Lewis Carroll, or at least he had access to them?"

"Let me think this over," the Pillar says. "The Cheshire kills girls who were born in villages around where Lewis Carroll lived. Not just that, but places where sandstones or statues of a grinning cat exist. What could that mean?"

"Like I said, I can't interpret the meaning, but this is no coincidence."

"And where is Constance from?"

My eyes widen. Why haven't I thought of that?

"Wait. You probably won't find that info on the net," he checks his phone, surfing some secret forum or something. "Just a minute," he keeps searching. "Here it is. Constance Richard," the Pillar stops in the middle of the sentence. "In London."

"So no connection to the other girls?" I feel disappointed. Another lost lead.

"Not necessarily. Who said there isn't a statue of a grinning cat in London? I just don't know of it. Your theory is still possible," the Pillar says.

The light above our seats flashes, urging us to fasten our seat belts. We've arrived.

"Now that we're about to land," the Pillar says. "There is something I have to do." He stands up and faces everyone in the plane. "Ladies and gentlemen, honored visitors of the Vatican City, may I have your attention?"

"Please sit down, sir," the flight attendant demands, but he ignores her.

"I'm the Archbishop of the Frabjous Christians of Monte Carlo," he says. I am sure there is no such thing. "And I'd like you to recite this little prayer with me before we land."

"Sir!" the flight attendant repeats to no prevail. "Please sit down! We're about to land."

"Do you think we can land without the will of God, young lady?" he says to her, and wins the passengers' attention immediately. "Do you think your seatbelts will save me from the wrath of God, if He so desires to crash this plane to pieces?"

The flight attendant shrugs, and the crowd begs the Pillar to recite his landing prayer. "Okay, just make it quick," she lowers her head and walks away.

"After me, please," he raises his hand to the plane's roof and begins, "Now I sit me down to land," and the passengers repeat after him, all in one voice. "I pray the lord with open hands," this has become the Vatican Airlines. "That if I die before we land," I can't believe how poor his rhyming is. Why are these people even following him? "Please don't take me to Wonderland!"

"Amen," everyone says, and I feel like I want to dig Lewis Carroll up from his grave and ask him who the Pillar really is.

Chapter 44

The Vatican City

Once we land, the Pillar stops a taxi and chirps in Italian. When I say chirp, I mean it. It's like he is someone else entirely when he talks this loud language. I listen to him the way he says *bene* and cups his finger like Italians do. The taxi driver is fascinated by the Pillar, although I can't understand what they are saying. All I know is the Pillar's name is suddenly Professor Carlo Pallotti.

We finally stop at a beautiful square with narrow streets. The Pillar takes me by the hand and shows me around. He says we're going to St. Peters, one of the oldest churches in the world.

"Basilica di San Pietro in Vaticano," he waves at the most beautiful church in front of us.

"Mama Mia!" I find myself saying. I am not mocking him. Truly, the whole place and the church are magical. I can't believe I have been trapped in the asylum for all this time. The world outside is mad, but it's also beautiful. If I weren't here on a mission, I'd be touring this location and taking pictures all day long. "But wait a minute, Professor Carlo Pallotti," I say. "What does this have to do with the White Queen?"

The Pillar doesn't answer me. He ushers me to some kind of a parade nearby. Not in the sense of carnivals and dancing girls. This is a very respectable celebration. All people look peaceful and modest. They seem to be waiting for someone, all looking in one direction. Carriages pass slowly between the spectators on both sides. It looks like the Queen of England's birthday parade, which I have just seen footage of on the plane.

The Pillar takes off his hat and tucks it in his suit. He tells me that there is a dress code for being near the basilica. Hats aren't allowed.

"So what are we waiting for?" I ask.

"We're waiting for her," the Pillar says, knocking his cane proudly against the ground. "The White Queen herself."

"I notice you haven't smoked since we came back from London," I remark, standing among the celebrating people.

"That's true," the Pillar nods. "Here is what you have to know. Of all enemies I have met in my life, I only respect one," the Pillar says, chin up, saluting other people waiting on the opposite side. "The White Queen." He nods his head toward a red carriage pulled by two white horses. It's filled with a number of nuns or priestesses waving solemnly at us and the people around. I feel like I have to bow my head and wave back. They are beautiful. Old. Wise. And their smiles are relaxing. It's as if they have no envy or anxiety in their hearts. I wonder why they don't send the likes of them to nurse us in the asylum, instead of Waltraud and Ogier.

Still, I don't think any of them is the White Queen.

"Vatican protocol formally requires that women, Catholic queens and princesses precisely, wear a long black dress with a collar, long sleeves and a black mantilla," the Pillar whispers in my ear as he salutes them with me.

"Mantilla? You mean that shawl on their heads?" I say.

"That's it."

"So are these women nuns or princesses?"

"Those are nuns. This is a very special ceremony," he explains. "Only a few selected princesses and queens were exempted and allowed to wear white in the course of the history of the Vatican."

"Really?"

"It's a very sensitive exemption," the Pillar explains. "Only a few queens, like the Queen of Belgium, Italy, and Luxembourg were given that privilege. They like to call it Privilege du Blanc, 'the privilege of the white,'" he says. "Of course, the most important woman who was ever exempted is her," he points at another carriage that appears. "She's both a nun and Wonderland's White Queen."

There is one woman in the carriage. She wears all white, her hair is white and smooth, and her face is gleaming with some invisible serene power. She isn't old like the others, probably in her late-thirties. Men and women nod at her as she waves at them. The way people look at her reminds me how people used to look at Mother Teresa years ago. The woman simply has my heart, and strangely enough I want to go to war for her. I feel like I have met her in the past buried behind my eyes.

"Her name is Fabiola," the Pillar announces. "The White Queen." For the first time, I see him bow his head when her carriage passes before us.

Chapter 45

St. Peters, Vatican City

We follow Fabiola to a hallway inside St. Peters. The Pillar tells me that its inner designs are one of the most renowned works in Renaissance architecture. When I look at all this from another angle, I am such a lucky mad girl, having been to one of the oldest universities and churches in the last couple of days.

"I need to ask this, Professor," I whisper in his ear, while we stand in line to kiss Fabiola's hands and receive her blessings. "I can accept that Wonderland is real and that its inhabitants live among us. I am even trying to accept that the likes of the Cheshire aren't malevolent childhood fantasies, but vicious monsters? What puzzles me is to accept them to be living all over the globe. Shouldn't all of this be happening at Oxford University where Lewis wrote his book?"

"When Lewis Carroll found out about the darkness lurking in Wonderland, he did his best to free its good people, and entrap its monsters," the Pillar says while greeting other tourists. He has an uncanny way with old ladies. They all giggle at him, even the nuns. "After Lewis locked the monsters in Wonderland, the rest of its inhabitants had to survive through incarnation and spells that allowed them to disguise behind new personalities all over the world. It was best for them to separate, so they wouldn't cross paths. No one wanted to be reminded of what happened there. But since Wonderlanders are frabjous people by nature, they excelled wherever they were. I won't be surprised if the Duchess ends up ruling England, the White Queen becomes the next Mother Teresa, and the Cheshire has a great chance to sell his soul to the devil. Those are a few of many others we haven't met yet," he nods at one more woman and it's our turn to meet the White Queen.

"In that scope, it's going to be a grand war between good and evil if the Wonderland Monsters escape like the Cheshire," I remark.

"It's called the Wonderland Wars, Alice," the Pillar says from the corner of his mouth, "Believe me, this is nothing compared to what you're about to see soon. Didn't you see me screaming on top of Tom Quad, warning people of an apocalypse? I hope you didn't think I was joking like the sane people did." The Pillar stands up and bows to Fabiola, then approaches her.

I watch the Pillar kneel on one leg and kiss Fabiola's hand. Last time, I didn't notice his hair is strangely spiky and short. It's also receding. He whispers something to the White Queen while on his knees. Like all other women, she smiles. Her smile is so serene, I swear I can feel light in my heart. But then when he raises his head and she takes a closer look at him, her face dims as if she has seen a ghost from the past.

Fabiola calls the ceremony to a halt and stands up. She is tall, and she is good-looking, really good-looking. Although I can't see the features of her body from underneath her white dress, I am assuming she has a body of a ballerina. The way she stands shows she is athletic. I wonder what made her take on the role of a nun when she could have been a superstar or model in this life.

The Pillar stands up and keeps talking to her. She throws a short glance at me over his shoulders. I smile at her, unable to do anything else. I have never seen anyone like her. She flashes a brief smile at me too. It's a sincere smile, but then she lets out a long sigh. Something about me brings sadness to her heart.

She turns back to the Pillar and whispers something to him. He nods agreeably. Then she holds the rim of her dress up like a princess and excuses herself from the other nuns who lower their heads with respect.

The Pillar approaches me in a hurry and pulls me by the hand to another private chamber in the church.

"What's going on? Aren't we going to meet the White Queen?" I wonder.

"We will. She doesn't want to meet me in public. I am a bad man, you know," the Pillar says in a regretful tone. I haven't heard him sound like that. What kind of effect does Fabiola have on him? On me?

We pass through an enormous arch as he nods at a couple of nuns guarding the huge doors to the chamber. They lead us into a new hall and close the doors behind us. Fabiola appears on the other end, and points at the confession booth.

"This is going to be my first time in a confession booth, " the Pillar says. "I hope it's big enough to fit us both."

Chapter 46

Confession Booth, St. Peters, Vatican City

"Forgive me Father for I have puffed," are the Pillar's first words in the booth. But then he looks embarrassed that he said that. It's like a habit. He doesn't feel comfortable inside.

We're waiting for the White Queen to open her screen to her compartment. The Pillar and I are squeezed into ours.

"Tell me what you want, Pillar," are her first words when she rolls the screen open. She sounds a lot more serious than I would have expected. "Make it short. You know your presence in the house of God isn't that welcomed."

"Insults aside, I need to ask you something about Wonderland," the Pillar says.

"There is no such thing as Wonderland," Fabiola says. I'm surprised with her response. I turn and face the Pillar with inquisitive eyes.

"She likes to joke," the Pillar explains.

"I'm not joking," Fabiola insists. "I don't talk about Wonderland in the presence of strangers."

"Alice is not a stranger," the Pillar says.

"She isn't *Alice*." The White Queen's tone isn't negotiable. Although I like her, I am surprised she denies everything. "Not the one you think she is."

"I'm Alice Wonder." I say. "And I don't necessarily want to be the 'Alice.' I am here to save a girl named Constance. Can you help us?"

The White Queen watches me closer from behind the screen. I see her eyes. They are a faint blue and the white around them, transparently clear.

"So it was really you who saved Constance the first time in Oxford," she considers. I think her heart warms toward me a little. "I saw it on TV."

"I thought you said the TV was the devil's window to the world," the Pillar arches an eyebrow.

"Don't speak until I permit you to," the White Queen says. Last time I heard this, the Pillar was saying it to the Duchess. "So back to you, Alice Wonder." She is definitely warming up to me. Saving lives means a lot to her. "You did a brave job there in Oxford."

"She couldn't have done it without me..." the Pillar's words are cut off by the White Queen's stare. He doesn't shrug, but he pouts. He could slit her throat. But then again, he couldn't. They have a crazy relationship.

"Come here, beautiful," the White Queen tells me. "Let me see you outside this booth."

I squeeze past the Pillar and get out, eager to meet her. Outside, she takes me by the hand and walks me along her private place for prayer. It's as artistic and holy as the rest of St. Peters.

"Brave girls aren't easy to come by these days," she still holds my hand, walking me to a part of the hall with statues all around.

"Thank you, White Queen," I nod, feeling safe in her hands.

"Please, call me Fabiola," she smiles at me and stops before an unusual part of the floor. It's made of black and white marble squares, and its surface glitters in the sunlight splaying through from the inlaid glass in the dome above us.

"Tell me why you want to save the girl," she says. "Is she related to you?"

"Not at all," I say.

"Why would you save someone you don't know?"

"I shared a special moment with Constance in Christ Church," I reply.

"Tell me about it," she pulls my chin up to meet her eyes. "Life's biggest moments are small moments."

"When she was in the fireplace, she refused to take my hand to save her at first," I say. "She only did when I told her my name was Alice. And then when I saved her, she hugged me so tightly, like no one ever has before. It was a new feeling for me."

"What kind of feeling?"

"I've always been looking for someone to help. At least, that's what I remember from my last week in the asylum."

"The asylum?" The White Queen gazes back at the Pillar as if he was my parent.

"I found her in an asylum. It's like a kindergarten for mad people, that's all," the Pillar shrugs his shoulder. "Trust me, she is *the* Alice."

The White Queen shakes her head and turns back to me. "Continue. You said you were always looking for someone to help."

"When I met Constance, I felt like she was helping me by letting me save her." The words flow without me even thinking about them. "It's hard to explain."

"It isn't hard at all," Fabiola says. "This is what true humans feel. We're all here in this world to help one another."

"And then Constance said something," I continue.

"Go on. I'm listening. What did the little girl say?"

"She said the Cheshire told her that Alice in Wonderland is now older and would be coming to save her. Constance has her room filled with drawings of me being Alice in Wonderland, and the Cheshire Cat told her I am coming to save her. Regardless of the craziness of all that, I had to promise her that I would never let the Cheshire hurt her."

"A promise is a serious matter, Alice," the White Queen nods.

"But I couldn't keep my promise," I say. "I wish to stay true to my word."

"That's something I can help with," she considers. "You see, most people who come to see me are broken. They need help. They think I can help them, when they only can help themselves. I try to make them understand that. In your case, you seem to know it. Only you can help yourself and keep the promise you made."

"I believe so..." I smile.

"I will help you. Not because of this horrible man you walk the earth with, but because of that great loving energy I sense coming from you toward the world." The White Queen has an unnamable magic on the tip of her tongue. The words she says stay with me somehow. It makes me feel twice as tall — which reminds me of Alice in the book again. "But I'm afraid you're not *the* Alice. You're not the one we're waiting for," she shakes her head. "I'm sorry. You have the same name and good heart, but not as strong as the real one."

Chapter 47

"Come here," the White Queen says, now that we're done with the Alice issue. "Give me a hug." I let her hug me. I feel the same way I did when Constance hugged me. I feel warmth, a surge of easiness, as if returning home. "The Pillar wants you to think you're the real Alice," she whispers in my ear so he can't hear. "He has plans of his own for Wonderland. Use him, but don't trust him." She pushes me away gently and holds me by the arms. "But I will help you save the girl."

"A chessboard-tiled floor," the Pillar breaks the whispering. I bet he is curious about what Fabiola told me. "I didn't know the nuns were into chess."

"It's not for chess," the White Queen says, winking at me. "I'll show you. Why don't you step on it, Alice?"

I comply right away, then stop before taking my first step. I remember I can't step on black tiles. My legs step on the white ones spontaneously, making my walking look awkward. But I finish the walk and end up on the other side.

The White Queen claps elegantly, barely making her hands touch. She looks at me as if I am an infant who just learned to walk. "The good at heart only walk on white," she explains, and now I know why I couldn't step on black in my cell.

"Oh," the Pillar says, taking a step away.

"Don't you want to try it, Pillar?" the White Queen teases him.

"I don't feel like playing Hopscotch today," he says, pretending to be checking the artistic design all around.

"So how do we catch the Cheshire?" I ask.

"Before you catch him, I need to tell you about the seven girls in the photographs," the White Queen says. "The Pillar sent them to my phone anonymously an hour ago," the Pillar never wastes time.

"Any ideas?" the Pillar asks her.

"Actually, yes," the White Queen says. "The theory you sent me is brilliant."

"It's my theory," I say.

"Don't be picky, Alice. We're a team now," he turns back to Fabiola. "But it's flawed. Constance wasn't born in one of the towns with a church that has a grinning cat statue in it."

"That's true," Fabiola says. "But it doesn't mean she isn't a perfect fit to the puzzle."

"I don't follow," I say.

"Most of the girls Lewis Carroll took pictures of have a significance in the events that happened in Wonderland," she explains. "One of those pictures the Cheshire requested is of a girl name Alice Westmaccott," she pulls out her phone and shows the photo to me. I have seen it before. This Alice isn't me. It's just another seven-year-old girl in a sepia-like photograph. "The name Alice was very common in Carroll's time," she continues. "This one is precisely the key to solve the puzzle of the seven girls."

"How is that so?" the Pillar asks.

"Alice Wesmacott's real full name is Alice Constance Richard Wesmacott."

"Okay?" I tilt my head, sensing a resolution coming my way.

"Alice Constance like a two-part name," Fabiola said. "Some people liked to call their kids with such names."

"So she could have been called Alice by some and Constance by others," the Pillar nods.

"Is that why Constance told me her mom wanted to call her Alice?" I wonder. "Was she giving me a hint?"

"I'm not sure about how much she knows about this," Fabiola says.

"This is mind boggling," the Pillar says. "The present day Constance didn't live a hundred and fifty years ago."

"That's true. But bear with me," Fabiola says. "The modern day Constance's name is Constance Albert Westmacott."

"She is a descendant of the Westmacotts." The puzzle starts to unfold for me. "But still, she wasn't born in a town with a Cheshire in a church."

"That's where you both missed it," Fabiola says. "Sir Richard Westmaccott was a well-known British sculptor in the time of Lewis Carroll. They knew each other well. His is commemorated by a blue plaque in his place of death in London."

"A sculptor?" I am trying to follow the complicated puzzle.

"Please don't tell me he is the one who carved all those grinning cats all over England?" The Pillar caught on faster than I did.

"Yes, he did," Fabiola said. "I know this because I talked many times with Lewis when he was obsessed with locking the doors to Wonderland in the past. He told me that each Wonderland Monster needed a special charm or magic to be locked away. He worked with Richard to trap the Cheshire."

"Let me get this straight," I am waving my hand over my head and walking around as I speak. "In order to trap the Cheshire, Lewis Carroll asked his sculptor friend, Richard Westmacott, to design those grinning cat statues. Each statue is in a town where at least one of the girls the Cheshire killed came from, right?"

"So far, yes." Fabiola nods.

"And Constance counts as one of the seven girls since she is a descendant of the man who sculpted those statues." I really hope I am making sense. "Now, the Cheshire is killing the girls because they're descendants of those girls in the photographs. I suppose there is a reason for it other than the carvings in their towns."

"So why is the Cheshire killing them?" the Pillar asks.

"I don't know," the White Queen says. "In all cases, they are the key to his freedom from whatever Lewis bestowed on him. All I know is where you can find the Cheshire at this time of year."

"And why haven't you said that from the beginning?" the Pillar rolls his eyes.

"In Belgium," Fabiola says. "A town called Ypres."

"Why would he be there now?" I wonder.

"There is a festival called Kattenstoet. The weirdest festival of all," Fabiola says.

"Are you talking about the Cat Throwing Festival?" The Pillar rubs his chin.

Fabiola nods.

"Cat throwing?" Again, I am having a hard time accepting things I hear.

"That's a long story," the Pillar cuts in. "We know what we came here for, and we better go now."

"Wait," the White Queen says. "I haven't yet told you why he attends the festival. I haven't told you why he has a grudge against humanity."

Suddenly, we hear voices outside. I hear someone thud on the floor, and a nun screaming briefly.

"What's going on?" I ask.

"Don't tell me it's the..." the Pillar exchanges looks with Fabiola.

"You didn't let them follow you here, did you?" Fabiola is suddenly furious.

"Who is it?" I can't stand not knowing.

"Who else? The Reds," Fabiola says. "You have to escape."

Chapter 48

Fabiola runs to a fireplace nearby and pulls an umbrella from inside—I think all Wonderlanders have a thing for fireplaces. It's a pink umbrella. It looks silly, and the color doesn't match the grand holiness of St. Peters. She throws it at me. "You will need it," she says as I catch it. "And when I say you'll need it, I mean it."

I want to ask if it's going to rain inside the basilica, but the situation is too dangerous for questions. The doors are pounding. The Reds who killed the nuns outside want in.

"And I believe you will need this?" she throws a hookah to the Pillar.

"Thank you for thinking of me, Fabiola," he smirks, catching it as the doors outside bang harder.

"As for me, I will need this," she pulls out a sword from the same fireplace. The sight of the White Queen with a sword in her hand confuses me. Since she's heard the pounding on the doors, she has turned into some warrior nun.

"What's that, Fabiola?" I wonder.

"It's the vorpal sword," she stares at her sword with pride. "Time to stand up to the face of evil."

I am the most bewildered Alice of all.

"Holy Borgroves!" The Pillar enjoys this, staring at Fabiola like she's a superwoman. The glimmer in his eyes is unpredictable. I think the Pillar feels something for the White Queen. "I miss the old days," he tells her.

"Don't get any ideas, Pillar," her words are sharp. "We're not fighting on the same side. We're only fighting the same enemy."

The three of us turn to face the doors. I can't help but feel like the worst twisted version of the Three Musketeers. The doors bang open. Finally, I will see the Reds.

Chapter 49

Tens of red hooded men with hollow faces rush in. Their hoods over their heads are heart-shaped, and most of them have Latin numbers sewn in gold on their back. The numbers vary from one to nine. They are the Reds, my new world's twisted version of Lewis Carroll's playing cards.

Some of the Reds have swords, some holds spears. None of them talk. They are here to kill us all. A brief thought runs through my head: why isn't anyone fighting with real guns? A spear swooshes next to my ear. I am not going to ask anymore.

"Lock the doors behind them!" the White Queen orders her nuns outside. "Trap them inside."

The Pillar whips his hose at the first hooded man approaching him. It's like he is Indiana Jones on crack. The hose snakes around the Red's hollow neck and chokes him. The Red falls to the floor in the form of an empty hood with no body inside. "Ace that!" the Pillar cheers and runs for another intruder.

Fabiola is surrounded by five of them, flashing her vorpal, and taking a fencing master's position. She even signals to them to approach her with her other hand, then pulls the hem of her white dress up again. I can't believe my eyes.

It only takes one of them to approach her before she goes nuts on him, stabbing and beheading him with the vorpal.

"The Vatican would be proud of you!" the Pillar cheers.

Fabiola is fast. She can walk briefly on air to launch her kicks, her veil floating behind her as if it's her swirling hair. When she spins her dress swirls with her, like a princess dancing underwater. She fights like a Samurai. Empty red hoods fall all around her.

"I never had a nun superhero when I was a child, you know that?" the Pillar tells me while choking a Red. "But then again, nuns and priests were not that fond of me."

"Shut up, Pillar," Fabiola says, still fighting. "I doubt you were ever a child."

I duck as another spear comes my way and hits the window. When I look outside, there are masses of people walking in prayer, holding candles and reciting hymns. They have no idea what's going on in here.

"In the holy name of Wonderland!" The Pillar chokes another Red to death. I catch his eyes while he enjoys his kill. But suddenly his face changes. He tosses his victim to the floor and runs on the church's banks toward me with that expressionless face again. It's like I am looking at death in his eyes. I don't know what's gotten into him, but I am paralyzed with fear again as he hops like a rabbit on the tips of the banks. He lands before me, pulls my head down and slashes his hose at one of the Reds who was about to kill me.

"If I were you, I'd start to use the privilege of having a Certificate of Insanity and kill some Reds." He takes a drag from his hookah, before he slashes the hose at another Red. "Look at them," he holds the hollow red hood in his hand. "They are the best kill. It's like they have never existed in the first place. A perfect crime."

"Stop talking and come and help me!" Fabiola demands from afar, still sword-battling a few on her side.

"She takes her job very seriously," the Pillar winks and runs off.

I kneel down and look at the red hood in my hand. I don't know what to with it, but it looks like I could use it. One of the Reds approaches me and I hit him with the umbrella between his legs. He screams in pain and his hollow hands reach between his legs. He lets out a big whiz then says, 'Jub Jub' in pain.

"Pull the umbrella tighter so the hook totally destroys him," the Pillar says, standing behind the podium now. I do, and the Red man falls to the floor like the rest. "Ladies and gentlemen," the Pillar shouts, his hands on the church podium. "I am Pillar the Killer. Approach me and I will go off with your heads." He adjusts his tie as he got the attention of most Reds darting his way. "Always wanted to say 'off with their heads' in a church," he murmurs and starts fighting.

I keep hitting Reds with my umbrella. It's one hell of a strong umbrella, but I am not sure Fabiola gave it to me for that purpose. In a flash, I find her behind me as she pulls me away. She stabs a number of Reds on the way as she tucks me into a confession booth. "It's better you stay here until this is over," she says.

I hold the door before she closes it. "Be careful, White Queen," I grab for her free hand. "I...I mean: we need you."

She smiles broadly, as if no one has ever appreciated what she does.

"I have to kill them fast," she says. "I have to attend prayers in a few." She slams the door behind her.

In the darkness of the booth, the screen on my left opens. A pair of curious eyes look through. They don't belong to the Reds, because these eyes have a face.

"Hey Father, are you there?" a boy says. I recognize the voice. It's the annoying and arrogant Jack Diamonds.

Chapter 50

"I am, my son," I do my best to sound like older folks.

"What's with your voice, Father? Ah, it must have softened from gazing at the holy face of the Lord," Jack says. He's dead serious. I didn't know he has this side to him. "Tell me Father. What does he look like?"

"Who?" I frown in the dark as I hear the battle taking place outside.

"The Lord, Father. I bet he is a cool guy, right?"

"How dare you even think to speak of the Lord?" It takes all the breath in my stomach to imitate such a voice.

"Oh, I am sorry." Jack's eyes are trying to see deeper through the dark. "You see, I came to ask your opinion on something. I am in love with a girl. Her name is Alice. Alice Wonder. She is awesome, like marshmallow awesome."

I don't say anything, or I will laugh. I am not affected by him saying he is in love with me. I don't even know him, and he is weird. Also, I think he is a player. Good-looking guys like him must have a lot of girlfriends.

"I am crazy about her," he says. "I mean, really. I have no idea why. You know what I think, Father? I think she is insane. Like, really insane. Tooty fruity insane."

"Then why are you telling me this?" I cough to hide my voice.

"I thought you could talk to her about me. Tell her that I am a great guy. All I need is a date with her."

A spear smashes through the confession room and hits the wall behind me, right behind my ear. I scream.

"Father? Seriously, something's wrong with your voice," Jack says.

"I'm not a Father, you annoying stalker!" I yell at him.

"Alice? What are you doing here in the Vatican?"

"I was going to ask you the same question," I bang the door open. Fighting the Reds is much better than talking nonsense to this Jack Diamonds.

"Use the hood," he tells me when we're outside.

"Can you just go?" I bang one of the Reds with my umbrella.

"Suit yourself," he says and puts on the Red's hood. "I'm going to disappear." He buries his face under the hood and turns hollow. He begins killing Reds with his bare hands. Jack fights in the strangest ways. He kicks and hits as if he is a Kung Fu fighter. A horrible one actually. It works.

I find the closest Red hood and put it on. What a genius idea. When I approach them, they think I am one of them and I keep hitting them with the umbrella. The White Queen and the Pillar are fighting on the other side of the church. They can't see me because of the angle, but I can hear their voices. There are a few Reds left alive. I don't even know who those Reds are.

Jack and I come back-to-back while fighting. "How do you know about that weird Kung Fu slash Samurai stuff?" I shout.

"It's not Kung Fu," Jack says. "It's None Fu. Short for Nonsense Fu. It's basically karate, jujitsu, Kung Fu, and every other fighting technique in the world. Some like to call it the Art of Nonsense." He kicks one of the Reds saying, "Aiya."

"Nonsense?"

"It's the way Lewis Carroll used to fight," he explains.

"You knew Lewis Carroll?"

"That's a long story," Jack turns around and faces me. "You look so hollow," He says.

"You too," I laugh. "You think that's why the Reds left?" Since we stopped fighting they were all gone, thinking we were part of them. They've probably run to Fabiola and the Pillar.

"Do you think we should kiss now?" he says.

"Heck no." What's wrong with this guy?

"I mean, we don't even see our faces. It wouldn't hurt to try to see if we could feel them."

"You're obnoxious," I pull away from him. "Why do you keep following me?"

"The heart has reason that reason doesn't know of."

"Oh, please," I wave my hands in the air. "Grow up. And please leave me alone."

The Pillar and Fabiola come running toward me. "One left to go and they're all dead," the Pillar is about to choke me with his hose.

"Wait. It's me," I take the hood off. "And him..." When I point to Jack, he's gone. I wonder if I was too harsh on him.

"That was a brilliant idea," the Pillar says, sitting on the bank and panting. "We could have just killed you."

"Don't listen to him, Alice." The White Queen salutes me. "It was a smart move. You're still learning. And I saw you give them heck. You are brave."

"Did you see how she killed some of the Reds Pillar?"

"And I thought it was 'thou shalt not kill," he sighs and stands up. "Come on, Alice, we have a plane to catch."

"I know," I can't even catch my breath in this fast paced Wonderland War. "We're going to Belgium to find the Cheshire."

"As a matter of fact, no," the Pillar says. "We're heading back to the asylum. It's late and if you don't show up there, Waltraud and Ogier will be suspicious. I don't want Tommy to be exposed. You're supposed to be in his care by morning. That's what he tells the underground ward."

"A hero by day, a loon by night," I mumble. "I hope I see you again Fabiola."

"I'm sure you will," she kisses me on the forehead. "Although you're not *the* Alice, I feel tremendous love for you since I met you. Now go. I have a prayer to attend, and thousands of people who shouldn't see me with a sword."

"Take care of yourself." I kiss her on the cheek.

"Can we just stop all the lovey-dovey moments and move on?" The Pillar pulls me by the hand. "Say 'hi' to God for me, Fabiola. Tell him I am sorry I smoked in his booth and killed in his church. Is there such repentance for that?"

"Stop," the White Queen says. "Let me tell you about the Cheshire's past first."

Chapter 51

Alice's Cell, Radcliffe Lunatic Asylum

Hours later, after Fabiola told us about the Cheshire, I am dreaming in my cell again. It's a dream about my boyfriend, Adam. He is still wearing his hood and I can't see his face. We're alone in Christ Church's garden.

"Am I insane?" I ask Adam, not sure why I do.

"It depends," Adam says.

"It depends?"

"On whether it's more important to know if you're insane, or to know who you are," he says.

"You're talking in riddles, just like the Pillar," I say to him.

"I am not the Pillar, Alice," he says. "I'm Adam. The love of your life."

"I still have a whole life in front of me. How do you know you're the love of my life?"

"I know you will never love someone the way you loved me."

"Why don't you show me your face then?" I wonder. "I need to see the face of the one I loved."

"You still love me, Alice," he says. "I'm still *madly* in love with you." He stops for a moment. "I'm not hiding my face from you. This is my face. Maybe it's just you who doesn't see me."

"Me?"

"I don't know why you do it, but it seems that you're not ready to see me." He sounds sincere. Again, I love his voice. It's reminds me of a lullaby I can't remember from when I was child—if that last sentence makes any sense. "I think you're afraid to remember me and then have to deal with my absence. My death was really hard on you."

"So I either remember you and a great pain comes with it, or forget you and great madness comes with it." I am evaluating my options.

"If forgetting me is going to make you happy, I don't mind," he says. "I see you have a thing for this boy you met."

"Boy? You mean Jack Diamonds?" I laugh. "No, he's a loon. I don't even know him, I swear."

"It's alright to meet other people after my death, Alice," Adam says. "It's really alright. I think he loves you dearly."

"What? How can you say so? I told you. I don't even know him. He is really weird. He doesn't even know me. I love you, Adam."

"You don't even remember me," he laughs from under the hood.

"I don't remember your face, but I remember you in my heart somehow," I say. "It's a feeling I can't escape."

"Then I will always be with you."

I say nothing. A tear trickles down my cheek. "Will you be with me when I face the Cheshire tomorrow?" I ask him to make sure he means it. Maybe spirits can still protect their loved ones after death.

"I will be, but there is something you have to know," he says. "The power the Cheshire is after is scarier than death itself."

"Do you know what it is?"

"I can't say. You have to figure it out. The power he is after surpasses any imagination. I mean *any* imagination. He will be the scariest face of evil in the world."

"You're scaring me, Adam."

"I am, because I care about you. If you're going after the Cheshire, you need to know the kind of danger you're facing. The Cheshire is going to perform a forbidden ritual tomorrow. You have to stop him, or..."

"Or?"

"It will be the end of the world."

"What kind of ritual, Adam?" I feel like waking up from my dream, but I try to do my best not to. The plants in Oxford's garden are drowning in water all of a sudden. A crazy flood swarms the university. Its tides are really high. Is this the end of the world Adam talked about?

When I open my eyes, I am all wet in my cell. Waltraud stands above me with a bucket of ice cold water. "*Vake* up, Alice," she laughs. "Time for some shock therapy."

Chapter 52

The Mush Room, Radcliffe Lunatic Asylum

Ogier rubs the two electrodes together as if he is a child with a fork and spoon in his hand. The spark he creates send shivers down my spine. I take a deep breath before the electricity reaches me, reminding myself that this is my new life. A hero by day, a mad girl by night.

Waltraud laughs each time I shake and shiver. She is still smoking her cigarette, watching me as if I were her favorite TV series. As electricity surges through me, I remember what the Pillar told me on the way back. He was talking about the easiest way to tell if someone is insane. It's not the way they look, talk, or behave. The most common trait in insane people is that they think they aren't insane. According to the Pillar's nonsensical logic, we're all insane. The only way to survive insanity is to admit it.

"You know that I am not being examined by a specialist when I leave every morning, right?" I tell Waltraud, still sweating from the buzzes. "You know I save lives in the outside world, don't you?"

Waltraud almost chokes laughing at me. "But of course, my dear Alice." She keeps on laughing with Ogier. "I also know you're a princess in the real world."

Ogier buzzes me again and all I can do is laugh with them. It's a hysterical moment. We all laugh, and we don't know why exactly. Am I laughing at the fact that there is no way in the world they'll believe me. Maybe I am laughing because I am really insane.

"Seriously," I hiccup between the laughs. "You must have seen me on TV. My picture was everywhere yesterday. I am the girl who ate a block of cheese in the Great Hall in Oxford University that morning."

"Cheeeeees?" Waltraud kills her cigarette on the floor. Every big thing in her body is vibrating from laughter. "Why did you eat the cheese, Alice? Are you a rat?" Ogier laughs at this part. Sometimes he reminds me of Frankenstein.

My laughing suddenly stops and I stare at them. They sound like they really haven't seen me. Could it be they never watch the news while living here in the underground ward?

"You seriously didn't see me?" My lips are dry when I say that. And my head is still buzzing.

"I think this is enough therapy for her today," Waltraud tells Ogier. "She is losing it." She tries to cup her hands over her mouth to keep from laughing.

"My God," I say. "You didn't see me."

"Of course, we didn't," Waltraud says. "Christ Church was closed yesterday. The police needed to collect evidence for the Cheshire murders. No students or tourists were allowed inside."

Chapter 53

The Pillar's Private Airplane - On the way to Belgium

It's early morning. We're on the Pillar's private plane, heading to the town of Ypres in Belgium. I am not surprised when I find out that his whimsical and speechless chauffeur is our flight attendant. But I am quite surprised when I learn he is also the pilot.

"I never knew you had a private plane," I say, sitting next to him in the comfortable seat as the private jet takes off. It looks like an exceptionally sunny day for this time of year. The Pillar says that the flight should only take twenty-nine minutes.

"You don't know anything about me, Alice," he surfs the internet on his phone, gathering more information about Kattenstoet. "If Tom Truckle is cheap with airplane tickets, then I'd rather use my plane. I have a hookah lounge in here."

"The Emirates Airlines also had a hookah lounge. You weren't impressed with it," I comment.

"Wonderland hookah is something else. Lewis Carroll will tell you about it one day," he tilts his head, offended by my comparison.

"And if I may ask, does your chauffeur have a name?"

"I never asked. I call him Chauffeur. Does he remind you of Ratatouille the anime?" he says nonchalantly. "He doesn't speak much, if you haven't noticed. He is dear to me. He works for free, as long as I protect him from the Cheshire."

"Cheshire? What would the Cheshire want to do with your whimsical chauffeur?"

"My chauffeur is very *mousy* if you haven't noticed. Cat and mouse aren't the best of friends," the Pillar winks. "Enough about him. You were telling me Waltraud and Ogier claim Christ Church was closed yesterday, right?"

"Yes."

"Then what do you call this?" he shows me the news coverage from TV on his phone. It shows all that happened, and the footage of me eating cheese in the Great Hall. "You're very famous on Youtube, by the way. Boy, you love cheese so much."

"So Waltraud is playing games with me, right?"

"Listen, Alice," the Pillar is impatient. "If you're going to question your sanity whenever someone tells you you're insane, you'll spend your life in misery. For instance, all this, including the video, could all be happening in your mind. Right?"

"You've got a point."

"Then how do you really know what is true and what is not?" he says. "A friend of mine called Einstein once said, 'Reality is merely an illusion, albeit a very persistent one.'"

"Einstein was your friend?" I narrow my eyebrows.

"And he's an excellent hookah smoker. He puffed faster than the speed of light, relatively speaking of course," the Pillar leans back in his seat. "How do you think he came up with his genius madness?"

"One last question," I say. "Why doesn't the FBI, Interpol, or any authority do anything about the killings? I mean, my picture is all over the world and no one interrogated me or bothered even finding me."

"Do you really want me to answer that?" the Pillar stares at the ceiling.

"Because I am mad?"

"That's a possibility of course, but not the real reason."

"Then what is it?" I am feeling helpless. "Are you working for the Interpol?"

"Me? Of course not," the Pillar chuckles. "Intercontinental, maybe. For two days, and they fired me for teaching customers how to smoke. Your problem is that you're always asking the wrong questions Alice."

"How so?"

"A sane person would want to figure out who works for the Interpol or the FBI," he says. "But an insane person would ask who the FBI, Interpol, and the British Parliament really work for."

I turn and pull out a magazine to read. I am not even going to go there and ask who the FBI works for. Let's just stick to the Cheshire's mystery.

"By the way," the Pillar says. "The grinning cat carving in St. Christopher in Pott Shrigly was stolen this morning."

Chapter 54

"What?" I put the magazine back. "Why didn't you tell me?"

"You're always asking, Alice. I thought I'd feed your curiosity first."

"The whole statue was stolen?"

"It wasn't a statue, but a grinning cat carved in the wall," the Pillar says. "It turned out this carving was removable. It's practically a mask, disguised as a carving in the wall. That Richard Westmacott was a genius."

"So what does this mean?"

"It means the Cheshire stole it," the Pillar says. "And it means your theory is right. Somehow, the Cheshire was after the one grinning cat carving in those churches that was secretly a mask. My bet is he didn't know which one it was. Knowing how Carroll implanted secrets in everything, I bet it took the Cheshire some time to steal the right mask without messing things up."

"What do you mean?"

"Carroll was meticulous. I am not surprised if stealing the wrong mask would have resulted in the destruction of all the other masks by some Carrollian magic."

"So the Cheshire has the power Lewis Carroll deprived him of now?" I am disturbed by even thinking about it.

The Pillar nods. He looks more annoyed with the Cheshire getting the power than concerned with humanity's fate. "The Cat is out of the bag. The White Queen said it wouldn't be good if he got that power."

"Adam told me the same thing in my dreams," I mumble. "He said it would be the end of the world."

"Adam, your boyfriend?" the Pillar says. I notice he's always focusing when I mention Adam.

"I dreamt about him last night. He mentioned the same thing the White Queen said," I explain. "That the power the Cheshire is acquiring is scarier than death itself. He also said the Cheshire needs Constance to complete the ritual."

"So that's it," the Pillar clicks his fingers. "The Cheshire needs them both, the mask and Constance to perform the ritual to get his power back."

"We could be too late."

"No, we're not," the Pillar says. "Think of it. Why did Adam show up in your dream just one day before the Kattenstoet festival? A festival about cats. Something in the festival completes the circle of the ritual. A mask, a girl, and a crazy event about people throwing cats out their windows. That's all it takes. It's a mad world out there."

Chapter 55

Grote Market, Town of Ypres, Belgium

The Cheshire, wearing one of his grinning cat masks, sat with a glass of milk in his hand. He was rocking back and forth in a chair to the song *Cats in the Cradle* by Harry Chapman. The view in front of him was enchanting. He was looking over the famous Grote Market in the Belgian town of Ypres. The sun was unusually present today, fighting against the stubborn snow. Everyone was preparing for the Kattenstoet festival.

He lifted his mask for a moment and took one last sip from his glass. It was a special brand of milk, exclusively exported from Cheshire County. He let the warm milk sweep down his throat and let out a purr. Then he put his grinning mask back on.

Lowering his hand, he pressed his fingers hard on the glass until it cracked. Red and white colors were spilled together on the parquet, and it felt good to him. Sometimes small things like breaking a glass were an even better release from the anger inside he suppressed for humankind. He let out an even longer purr, waving through the opening in his orange mask.

Behind him, in this abandoned Renaissance hotel, a girl lay tied on the floor. She was young, about ten years old. Unlike his other victims, she didn't have a grin sewn to her mouth. She's been there for some time. She wasn't dead yet. She was very special, and he needed her.

The Cheshire gazed briefly at the antique mirror next to him. It was old, wrapped up in spider webs and dead butterflies caught by the spiders themselves. But still he could see his masked face. He looked silly in this mask, he thought. He missed his face. His real face. Most of all, he missed his Cheshire Power, the one Lewis Carroll took from him. It was time to get it back.

None of that was the reason he broke the glass of milk. He loved milk. It was his favorite thing in the world. The worst thing in the world was humans. He could not forget or forgive what they had done to him in this town when he was a kid.

The Cheshire, possessing an old woman's body for now, turned to look down from his French window. An old woman was a great disguise, in case he needed to take off his mask. He looked down upon the arriving tourists ready to celebrate.

Everyone in this Flemish part of Belgium talked in a language he hated most, French. They were on top of his human-hate list. The Cheshire hated how the French ate raw meat without cooking it, like cannibals. He hated the way they pronounced his name with an accent: Che-cha-ree, it sounded uncannily close to "Cherie" in French, which meant "sweetheart." The Cheshire didn't want to be anyone's sweetheart. He didn't want to think of having a heart. What he hated most about the French and the Belgians was the memory they brought back. That harsh memory that made him crack the glass of milk and never care about his bleeding hand.

The memory was about this town, Ypres. It was many centuries ago, when they started killing, throwing, and burning cats in Europe. A long time before he fled to Wonderland.

People thought that cats died young, but they were immortal spirits. Wonderland was an unknown place then. It was a long time before Lewis Carroll and the Cheshire turned into enemies in a chessboard game called life.

The Cheshire closed his eyes, took a deep breath, and remembered the first time cats were massacred in front of his eyes...

Chapter 56
Ypres, Belgium 15ᵗʰ Century

He was a kid. A happy, furry, tail wiggling, and purring cat like the others. He had just stopped getting food and milk from his mother a week ago. His dad wasn't fond of his laziness and urged him to go out and start hunting for food. Cheshire wasn't fond of killing animals, but he had to eat.

"Rats, my son," his mother purred. "That's our best food."

"But they are horrible little creatures, mommy," he said. "I mean, I get so grossed out by their noses and whiskers."

"I hate them too."

"Then why do you eat something you hate?" He always thought it a physiological defect of his kind to eat something they hated. What was wrong with butterflies? They looked lovely and he loved the way they crunched between his teeth. Surely they were hard to catch, but that was why he was fond of caterpillars. They were slow and full of vitamins, since all a caterpillar did was eat. They were like raw butterflies, something the French would love--there was no room in his memory for remembering how the French ate frogs. Holy paws and purrs, why frogs? The Cheshire used to love them when he was a kid. The way they hopped everywhere, it was like they were kangaroos for humans.

But the Cheshire ended up hungry, so he began to hunt for himself.

Ypres was a small town by then, known for exporting clothes to England. They had that huge clothes tower where they kept the clothes for months, before they were shipped away. Rats loved it and were fond of the tower, so humans encouraged cats from all over town to visit and eat the rats.

In general, many Europeans didn't love cats around the sixteenth-century. Cats were associated with witches, and were said to be inhabited by demons and devils. But the clothes tower, that was the exception.

The first time the Cheshire went there, he saw a cat rolling a dead rat with its paws and playing with it. He thought it was mean to kill someone and play with their corpse. A dead human was honored by burial or cremation; a rat's corpse should have been eaten right away in that context.

"I am not playing with it," the other cat said to Cheshire. "I'm checking it for diseases. Rats are stinky. They spend their time in sewers and other people's cheeses."

The Cheshire wasn't going to go through that conversation again. Why did they eat them then?

It only took him a week before he turned into a rat serial killer. It was his first form of serial killing then. The rats tasted horrible, but gave him energy to run around and play all day. The townspeople began giving fish spines to the cats as a reward for killing the rats, as long as the cats only went to the clothes tower and not all over town, especially to the Grote Market, where humans had their groceries.

One day, the Cheshire's father brought his dead uncle's corpse to bury it. He was killed by the townspeople with a pan on his head for padding into the Grote Market. It was the Cheshire's first epiphany about how humans hated his kind--of course people now cherish cats and pet them, but that wasn't the case then.

It was rumored there was a man with a pipe and pied clothes who could tempt rats out of any town. He played the devil's music with his flute and the rats followed him out of town. If he had come, the cats would have been out of food and business.

The Cheshire's father was one of the first to go negotiate with the man whom everyone called the Pied Piper. Cats from all over Belgium and France traveled to meet the Piper. They begged him not to come to Ypres, or they'd be out of food. The Cheshire accompanied his dad that day.

After hours and hours of pondering, the Piper agreed not to come to Ypres. He remarked that his absence would make him lose a lot of money, since rat catching was a hot business at the time. So he made a deal with the cats that some of them had to sell their souls to him. He told them that demons and rogue spirits were lost in the cerebral realms of the world and needed a body to inhabit. Cats were the perfect host due to their agility and smart moves. The Piper promised that it wouldn't change who they were as cats. In fact, it might make them stronger. Reluctantly, a number of cats agreed and were never seen again. Although the Piper had his eyes on the Cheshire that day, his father rejected the idea furiously, taking his son back to town.

Months later, a series of crimes and unexplained phenomenon soared all over Europe. They were mostly connected to witches. In the town of Ypres, everyone believed witches performed their sins through cats.

Suddenly, the clothes tower was shut and fanatics began catching cats and throwing them from windows to kill them. It had become a new hobby, encouraged by parents and practiced by children.

But the cats were as flexible as yoyos. No amount of throwing killed them, only an unexperienced few died. And then in one of humanities' most absurd incidents, the Flemish townspeople, the raw meat eaters, gathered and decided to rid their town from the cats who supposedly caused all their misery. Instead of investigating what they did wrong as humans, it was the cats.

As punishment, a parade and festival was run for days. The townspeople lured the cats to the clothes tower and caught them. They packed them into sacks and threw them from the highest towers down to the ground. A cat's landing skills and balance were useless when crammed into a sack. It needed space to curl its body in order to land without being hurt. Also the heights were now unimaginable.

The Cheshire twitched with the broken glass of milk in his hand. The memory was too gory to imagine. Thousands of fluffy creatures, forests of outstretched arms, flying in the air with no parachutes on their backs. The townspeople hailed and clapped, while they cussed the devils and demons that they thought inhabited those cats, they smiled while cat blood was spattered on the streets of Ypres. He continued his memory, remembering the day when he and his family was caught and killed.

Chapter 57

One day, the Cheshire's family was caught: mother, father, sisters, brothers, and even him. They were packed into the sack, left in the darkness to die, wondering when they would hit the ground. When a human pulled the sack to crush it all the way down, the Cheshire pleaded all he could. He meowed, purred, and screamed. He hung with his claws upside down, thinking the humans might have mercy on him. But no mercy was given. The Cheshire cried so hard that the Gods gifted him with the power of speech for a moment.

"Help us!" the Cheshire pleaded, his eyes widening at the miracle.

"Did you hear that?" one of the humans asked the other who was holding the sack. "I think the cat just begged for help."

"It did?" the one who held the sack wondered, and the whole Cheshire family felt hope.

"It's me, the Cheshire," he shouted in his tiny voice. "Please. You don't have to do this."

"It really talks," one said, "The damned cats are possessed by the devil. Throw it!"

And with that, the Cheshire's sack sank free-falling into the air. With his family panicking all around him, the look of death painting their faces, the Cheshire felt an unstoppable need for revenge. An unstoppable need for killing everything that is human. His small claws sharpened and kept slithering at the sack from inside. A little before his family died, splashing to the ground, the Cheshire saw sunlight burning his eyes through the holes he'd created. He slid through them like cats do and jumped, landing on his paws, then used his balance center inside his ears to control the movements and not die.

That day, he stood in his place as the sky kept raining cats. Each time their blood splashed onto his face, his grin widened. Each dying cat was his fuel for the apocalypse he was going to bring onto humans of the world later. To do that, he had to gather an army of monsters. Later in the years, he knew he could find plenty of them in Wonderland.

Right now, the Cheshire walked with his human feet over the scattered glass. He knelt down next to the captive girl wondering how she'd look with a grin sewn to her face. But he couldn't do that to her now. After many trials and errors, this was the girl he needed to get back the powers.

"Soon I will perform the ritual," his voice sounded muffled behind the mask. "Soon, Carroll. Then I will have the scariest face in the world. The face that is not a face. I will have the one power that will make me invincible." His power was the kind of power no one could think about. It was smooth, yet deadly. To get it, he had to use Constance, one of the descendants Carroll photographed. If only the world knew that these photographs weren't just a hobby, that each one held a secret within it.

But the world was ignorant and pompous, like always. The Cheshire was going to teach them their last lesson ever. Let's see who has the last grin.

Chapter 58

Kattenstoet Festival, Ypres, Belgium

The Pillar and I are licking ice cream at Il Gusto d'Italia, one of the most famous places in Ypres. It's not like we've come here for the ice cream, but licking it while staring at the madness around us is the best way to hang onto sanity.

The Kattenstoet parade is immense. Many people, a lot of them children, come from all over the world to celebrate that crazy day. It's only seconds before we're pushed among the crowd, urged to walk ahead in the parade. In my modern day Alice outfit and the Pillar's blue suit, we look like freaks. People are either dressed as cats, wearing feline ears, hanging cat's tails or meowing like cats. Girls have whiskers drawn on their faces, and elders have Mickey Mouse cat ears on, along with other medieval clothes and accessories. It's beautiful actually, only if it didn't represent a horrible memory of killing cats.

"This place is nuts," I laugh, holding the umbrella Fabiola has given me. She told me I will need it, but I still don't know how.

"Every dog's dream," the Pillar puffs his pipe. He doesn't look happy. All he is looking for is a sign to spot the Cheshire.

Among the parade, we pass by a famous clock tower where it shows the time is three in the afternoon.

"Ding dong, something is wrong," the Pillar says.

I don't know what he means, but we come across the belfry where a huge bell rings and people start to throw candy in the air.

Colorful marching bands begin to fill the square in front of the famous clothes tower, where the Cheshire family has probably been thrown out in the past--the Pillar educated me all about it this morning. He had his chauffeur research the Cheshire's background in Ypres.

More children dressed in feline costumes make clawing gestures, while elders twirl the flag of a Flemish lion. It's Ypres's national shield. How ironic, I think. A lion on the flag where they killed the same species in the past.

"Balloons!" I cry out like a little child. Huge balloons gather and take the shape of one huge cat in the sky.

I see young girls march next to us. They are dressed as Cleopatra as a tribute to Egyptian cats, which were considered Gods back then. Viking-costumed flutists follow them with dancing girls in blonde braids as a tribute to Celtic cats.

Things look ordinary, until Alice spots horses drawing a wagon of a caged witch who is acting as if she is pleading not to be burned. She is holding onto the bars and flipping her stiff black hair.

"Gotta love humans," the Pillar blurts out as he still looks for the Cheshire.

"Why? What's going to happen to the witch?"

"In the Grand Finale of the party, they are going to burn her," the Pillar pushes a couple of cat-clothed kids away. "Woof. Woof," he blows at them. "Of course, they won't burn the girl herself. They will burn a feline version of her. Can you believe this is the twenty-first century? People still believe that cats and witches are the cause of their misery."

Then I am distracted by a huge carriage made of feline fur. It looks like a huge red cat with scary jaws. They call it The Cradle. Children cheer seeing it and start climbing on the top and sides. I wonder if the huge cat on wheels is just hollow from inside, because it's big enough to have a dining table and chair inside. For a moment, I ponder if the Cheshire is hiding inside.

"And here comes Garfield," the Pillar points his cane at someone in a Garfield costume, walking next to a Puss in Boots.

I try to act as the Pillar, not worry, and enjoy the parade for a while. The buildings all around us are a work of art. The houses are Renaissance style, and the fact that there is almost no place to take a step makes me happy. Again, for a girl just out of an asylum, this is Heaven.

Suddenly, the parade stops as we're approached by a huge number of Pro-Cat activists. They are holding big animal rights signs, protesting against the cruelty that has been imposed on the cats of Ypres in the past. Their voices are loud and angry. I find myself pushed to the first row with the Pillar next to me. When I get a closer look at the Pro-Cat activists, fear prickles on the back of my neck. The Pillar holds my hand for assurance. What we're looking at might be normal for others, but not for us. All the activists in front of us wear the same exact orange mask on their face. A face of a grinning cat, just like the mask the Cheshire Cat had stolen from Pott Shrigly.

Chapter 59

"Ding dong...something is wrong," the Pillar says again, staring at the activists.

"You think he is one of them?" The thought of me staring at the Cheshire without knowing him is unsettling. He could easily be anyone in this masked crowd. I'd rather face a devil I know than one I don't.

"Brilliant isn't it?" The Pillar looks angered by the Cheshire's trick. "He has an unstoppable need to attend the festival and perform the ritual. Now, with all those masks, there's no way to know who he is. He's mocking us again."

"Shouldn't that mean that Constance is here?"

"In many ways, it does," the Pillar says as the activists make way for someone approaching from the back. It looks like their leader, a man dressed in a Pied Piper's costume. He holds a flute in his hand, a dossier, and has a few cat grinning masks with him.

"This is a peaceful protest," he raises his hands and talks to the people. I notice he is in his fifties and his face is heavily lined, as if he's been a big drinker or smoker in his younger days. He has a good tan though, and he is not wearing a mask. "All we ask is that you let us pass to the clothes tower to mourn our cats."

The people behind us murmur. They are wondering if there is enough space for them to walk through. They wouldn't want to spoil the parade, as they still have the need to move forward and continue the celebration.

"I have a couple of masks for those of you who have had a change of heart and want to mourn the many cats that have been killed in this town," the Piper grins, imitating the masks. "Have you ever had a cat, young lady?" he addresses me, bowing his head as he is a bit too tall.

"I think so." I don't remember having one.

"Was here name Dinah?" The Piper's grin continues as the Pillar tenses. I shrug, not knowing what's really going on. Has the man exposed me, or is he just referring to Alice's cat in the book? "Forgive my surreal sense of humor, but you look fabulous in this modern day Alice outfit," the Piper says.

"Does it really show?" I am beginning to worry like the Pillar. My outfit shouldn't really make someone think that way all at once.

"Please be one of us," he stretches out his long-fingered hand. "You must care for cats the way we do. This celebration is all wrong. We need to educate people that harming cats is unacceptable. It's a crime that deserves the death chamber, like killing human beings."

"We have appointments," the Pillar breaks in. "We love cats. Meow. But I am afraid she can't come."

The Piper turns to face the Pillar and I sense darkness in the air. Is it possible that this tall, tanned man is the Cheshire? Why is he dressed like a Piper, and not disguised among the others behind a mask?

The Piper and the Pillar stare at each other for a long time. I am starting to think this isn't the Cheshire, or the Pillar would have recognized him. I am puzzled all over again. I wish the Pillar wouldn't keep so many secrets from me.

"Professor Carter Pillar, I assume?" the Piper utters finally.

My heart drops to the floor.

"Do you know me?" the Pillar asks, and I am confused again. What's going on?

"It's a pleasure to meet you," the Piper stretches out his hand and shakes the Pillar's warmly as the grin on his face disappears. "I was told I might find you in the parade. In fact, I have two masks and tickets for you to join the Pro-Cats activists. I have heard a lot about your work. I hear you support cats, and love them dearly." I know the Pillar hates cats. "I heard about your great work in the field of *Kittycology*."

"Kittycology?" I know this is a joke, but I don't know what's happening. The Pillar knows it too, but he plays along. He likes games.

"And who told you about me, if I may ask?" The Pillar drags from his pipe, glancing at me from the corner of his eye.

"Mr. Warrington Kattenstoet, of course. He is the Director of the Pro-Cat activists. Unfortunately, he couldn't make it today," the Piper hands us the masks and tickets. "But he insisted it would be an honor if you and your daughter would accompany us."

I take my mask reluctantly as the Pillar secretly winks at me. He puts his mask on, accepting the invitation. The name Warrington Kattenstoet is a big joke. Warrington is where Lewis Carroll was born, and Kattenstoet is the event we're attending. The Cheshire is here and he wants us to play one of his games. He is inviting us to his ritual.

"And what should we call you?" the Pillar asks, as we cross over to join the Pro-Cats.

"Call me Piper for now," he smiles.

"I am curious why you're dressed like a Pied Piper at an event about cats," I have to ask.

"It's an in-house joke, young lady," he shakes his head. "In the Pro-Cats community we think the Piper must have been a cat. Who better to call when your town is rat-infested? The Piper. He does the same job cats do in terminating the rat race."

"Oh," the Pillar and I gaze each other. We look silly in these masks.

"I know all the stuff about the flute and such, but after the Piper tempted rats out of Hamlin, what do you think he did with them?"

"I heard he drowned them in the river," I respond.

"Not true, young lady," he protests. "He ate them, of course. Just like ancient people of this town sent the cats to kill the rats in the clothes tower. Now, follow me. As we walk amid the tourists to the clothes tower, the Pro-Cats start singing a song:

Pussycat, pussycat, where have you been?

I've been up to London to visit the Queen.

Pussycat, pussycat, what did you there?

I frightened a little mouse under her chair!

I have my mouth open wide under the mask when I hear that. The Pillar does nothing but end it with a high note, shouting, "Meow!" He says it as if he's saying "Amen."

Chapter 60

We pass through the crowd as they let us into the clothes tower. They agree we can use it, only for an hour, then leave so other tourists can use it. We step up. As we do, the Piper gives us mid-sized boxes with metallic hands on top. They are mildly heavy, and something is rocking it from inside.

"There are cats in these boxes," the Pillar says as we climb the stairs. I can hear a meow out of my box.

"Why cats?" I hiss at him. "It doesn't make sense. They are Pro-Cats. They won't be throwing them off the tower like other tourists."

"Other tourists don't throw real cats from the tower," the Pillar corrects me. "They throw stuffed cats as part of the event. Maybe the tower is like Noah's Ark. The Cheshire is going to drown the world with some flood, so he decided to save as many cats as he can." I know the Pillar is being sarcastic. He has no clue what we're up to, and I don't like the anticipation.

"He didn't invite us here for nothing," I remind him. "He wants to show us his power. My guess is the ritual is taking place atop the tower. This means Constance is here."

We reach the biggest room and each activist walks toward the row of cloistered windows looking over the parade and the whole town. They turn and face the inside of the circle, where the Piper stands.

This is definitely the ritual.

"Since the time we have here is short," the Piper says. "I will try to make this quick." One of the boxes rattles from inside. The rattling is unusual. The cats must be big. I hear mine clawing at the inner walls of the box. "I know all of you have lost ancestors to the incident that happened here many centuries ago when they killed them mercilessly, throwing them out of the windows."

Now, this makes more sense. Each and every one here is originally a cat, now in a human soul. They are here to avenge their ancestors. Being here is scary. I don't dare to even look at the Pillar. We've been ambushed.

"They also burned our ancestors in France a century later," a cat-masked woman says.

I read about cat burning in France on the Internet. Apparently people had a lot of grudges towards cats in that time.

"Not just France," another man raises his voice behind the mask. It's really hard to know who is talking and where the voices are coming from. "They killed cats in Brazil, too. My entire family was murdered."

"My family was murdered in Ancient Egypt. We were supposed to be Gods!" a third one says.

"I know we were Gods in this world before," the Piper calms the others. "The human holocaust on cats in the fifteenth-century didn't succeed anyways. We've always evolved and learned to survive. Some of us are tigers or lions. And most of you survived by stealing the breath of infant humans and taking their souls." He fists a hand and raises it in the air. I suddenly notice it's not a hand. It's a claw in a human body.

I remember one of the Mushroomers say that he wasn't mad. He said a cat had stolen the souls of his kids when they were young and no one believed him. What happens is that the kid dies and the cat grows up in a new human body of its choice. The Mushroomer said that cats live among us everywhere. I thought he was crazy. I don't know of anyone who'd believe what's happening right now if I told them.

"We should have never let humans domesticate us," the Piper says. "But history is full of mistakes. And on rare days like today, we get our revenge."

Everyone around us hails the Cheshire.

"The Cheshire has been through a lot, but he has always fought for us. He was fooled by Lewis Carroll when he locked him in Wonderland many years ago," the Piper says. "But like the Red King and Queen said in the books, how could they behead a cat with no head?" The Pro-Cat activists, or should I say cats, hail again. "The revenge the Cheshire has promised is closing in. Lewis stole the Cheshire's power after he couldn't lock him in Wonderland like the others."

"When is he getting his power back?" an activist asks.

"Patience, my friend," the Piper says. "The awful Lewis Carroll hid it in one of the sculptures of grinning cats all around the world. He then asked his friends to sculpt as many grinning cat statues and carvings as possible to elude the Cheshire Cat, so he could never get it back."

"What's in the mask?" an activist asks.

"What else, my friend," the Piper says. "His grin. The famous Cheshire Grin holds his power."

I know the Pillar and I can't wait to know the rest. But this is getting so surreal; I'd rather believe I am insane. This is all about the Cheshire getting his grin.

"The power in the mask was bonded with one of the girls Carroll took photographs of," the Piper continues. "The power was in the mask, but the key to unlocking it was in one of those girls' souls. All the Cheshire had to do was to kidnap the girl, suck her breath like cats do, and then take her soul. He made them look like murders to elude any Wonderland enemies out there. Six souls had been killed with no success, but the seventh must be it. And she is here with us today."

My eyes dart around looking for Constance, as the activists ask where and who the girl is.

"Her name is Constance," the Piper says. "And within a few moments the Cheshire will perform the ritual when the clock ticks 'brillig.'"

"What is brillig?" one asks, and I too found myself wanting to know.

"Brillig is four o'clock in Carrollian language," the Piper explains and then recites a small line from Carroll's most whimsical poem, the Jabberwocky, "'It was brillig, and slithy troves.'"

I miss the Pillar explaining these things to me. He hasn't talked since we came here. All he cares about is spotting the Cheshire. And all I can do is crane my neck to look at the clock tower afar. It's only ten minutes to brillig.

Chapter 61

"The ritual is simple," the Piper says. "When the clock ticks four, the Cheshire will appear and suck the girl's soul wearing the one and only Carrollian mask that holds his power."

"Meow!" The Pillar finally breaks lose, shouting from the top of his lungs. Crazily enough, all the other activists follow him. He doesn't look at me and I can't interpret his face.

"There will be one last thing needed to complete the ritual," the Piper says. "In order for the Cheshire to regain his power, he will need our help."

Everyone says they'd do anything for him. The Cheshire literally has a following.

"I know you'd do anything for the Cheshire, but it will be of great satisfaction for you as well," the Piper says. "Because today you get to avenge your ancestors! Now open your boxes, please."

The Pro-Cats begin opening their boxes and pulling out the cats, which aren't really cats. They are small tigers. Not the cute ones you see on TV, but viscous ones, ready to sink their fangs into anything that moves. Somehow, they are obedient to the Pro-Cats. They are held in small cages that the Pro-Cats ready to throw out of the window overlooking the parade attendees. The Pillar and I have no choice but to pretend we'll be doing the same, then we stare back at the Piper.

But the Piper is gone.

Instead, there is an old woman holding Constance in her grip. I know she is an old woman from the look of her body and her white hair flapping behind the mask. She raises her arms and shows her claws then nears them to Constance's neck.

"It's the Cheshire," the whole room snaps. They snap out of happiness, not fear.

"I wonder if Jesus Christ got that kind of attention," the Pillar mumbles next to me.

The Cheshire's presence is even scarier than the Pillar's. Scarier than the scariest thing I have ever seen, even that scruffy bunny in the mirror. It's as if I'm looking at death and can do nothing about it. He is so confident, even if he is hiding in the body of an old woman. He doesn't need to speak. He doesn't even need to show us his face. I think the unbearable fear I see on Constance's face is mirroring mine. The poor girl doesn't recognize me because of the mask I am wearing. I am torn between just running and crashing into the Cheshire, or waiting until I see a window of opportunity to do something more effective. It puzzles me why the Pillar is stranded when it comes to the Cheshire.

The heck with it. I take a deep breath before I run recklessly toward Constance to save her. God only knows what the consequences may be.

Chapter 62

The Pillar holds me tight before I run. He doesn't say anything. His grip is just too strong, kicking me back into reality. If I attack the Cheshire, neither Constance nor I will survive. We have two minutes left. I need to find another way.

"Once before, they threw us from the top of this building," the Cheshire woman says behind the mask. I am still puzzled about him being a woman. I imagine it's the human soul he chose to steal, but why an old woman? So he'd fool everyone? "Now, we'll show humankind what it means to have cats falling from the sky. Big cats this time. Vicious cats who will eat at them one by one. These cats in your hands will kill them, their wives, and their annoying children with red balloons everywhere. Just the way they killed us." The old woman's voice peaks. For a moment, I think I know the voice, but I can't recall it.

The Pro-Cats pull the lids open to allow the cats out. These cats have no fear. They stand ready at the edges, ready for the clock tower to strike four.

I almost hear the ticks in my heart. The Pillar said I am supposed to save lives. Now I am torn between the ones down below on the street and Constance. My God, the fear in her eyes is killing me already.

Tick. Tock. Almost four o'clock.

I pull my hand away from the Pillar, and ignore his voice when he says I should wait.

"I know now why you need me," I whisper to the Pillar. "You can't face the Cheshire by yourself." I decide I will go for Constance if there is no other choice. I can't let the Cheshire have her soul. Before I attack, the Cheshire does something I didn't see coming. He pulls his orange mask off and prepares to put on the Carrollian one from Pott Shrigly. In that brief moment, he, or she, is without a mask. I see the old woman's real face.

It's someone I know. How in the world didn't I see this coming? How in the world did the Cheshire fool and mock me this way?

I swallow hard and fist my hand to stay as calm as possible. The Cheshire is the old woman from the Great Hall. The woman with the grin who told me about the teacups.

Chapter 63

"And the madness begins," the Piper stands next to his locked box by the window. I am really concerned about his helplessness when it comes to the Cheshire.

The clock rings four o'clock.

"Revenge time!" the Cheshire says in his woman's voice. He sounds like a wicked old witch and signals for them to throw the big cats.

"It's raining cats," the Pillar raises his cane, pretending to be one of them. "Hallelujah."

At this moment, I realize that the Pillar really doesn't care about humans. With all his powers, he hasn't stopped the activists from their wrongdoing. His hate for the sane world is so real, it's scary. The only difference between him and the Cheshire is that he is temporarily on my side. The White Queen was right when she told me not to trust him.

I pull my mask away and run toward the Cheshire. "Hold on, Constance!" I yell as I wave the umbrella against him. The Cheshire grabs onto it midway, grins at me, and says in his female voice, "Haven't I told you we're all mad here. I remember I did more than a century and a half ago."

I am sweating as I try to push harder with my umbrella, but it's not working. He is much stronger than the Reds. His grin makes me doubt myself. I glance at Constance for a brief moment, afraid she'll be disappointed with me. I promised I'd save her.

The Cheshire pushes me harder to the floor, and I fall on my back and lose the umbrella. Behind me I hear screams from below. God knows what kind of massacre is happening in the parade. I hear women and children screaming, and big growling cats sinking their fangs in their flesh. The Pillar doesn't do anything when it comes to the Cheshire. He is standing there watching. Some of the activists recognize him as an intruder, and now he suddenly has to defend himself.

"Time for me to get my powers back," the Cheshire woman roars. She is holding Constance by her neck and has the grinning mask in the other hand. A lightning bolt strikes somewhere in the distance as she inhales deeply.

I stand up, run into her again, trying to knock her over. She slashes her claws at me and sends me back to the floor. Her claws cut through my pullover, and I am bleeding from my left arm.

"No one can stop me from what righteously belongs to me," she grins at me, while the Piper brings more boxes for the activists to throw on the parade. "You don't know what this power is, do you?" Her grinning is constant, and she enjoys showing it to me. I have a feeling that this is personal. Not just between the Cheshire and the humans, but between him and me. I wish I could remember the past.

"What is it?" I shout, as a snowy wind whizzes through the tower. I'm trying to stall the Cheshire by making useless conversation. "Tell me what Lewis took from you."

"My nine lives," the woman laughs. "My priceless nine lives. Once I get them, I will be immortal."

"But they are only nine lives," I am stalling, watching closer for a weakness in the Cheshire's woman body. "Not all that much."

"Oh, they are more than enough. If you only knew," she lifts the mask up and puts it on. "It's time to get back my grin, the one Lewis stole from me." The mask begins sparkling like stars. "Lewis bonded the grin with Alice Constance Westmaccott's soul by photographing her," the Cheshire is proud to tell me all about it now. Why not, when he is only seconds away from getting what he wants? "They weren't joking when they said that photographs captured the soul. Lewis was a genius and invented that kind of camera long ago. Luckily, Alice Constance Westmaccott passed her bond down to her descendants. Now, all I have to do is suck out this girl's soul and retrieve my powers." He means Constance. I watch him pull her closer to him. Behind me the world is in chaos, and the Pillar is in a vicious war with the activists. He's killed a lot of them, but there are too many.

The Cheshire is about to suck Constance's soul the way a cat sucks an infant's breath in real life.

Chapter 64

Although I am bleeding, I have no choice but to run and bump the Cheshire again. This time I close my eyes briefly, and try to remember what Jack Diamonds told me about the art of None Fu. He said that only if I believe in the power of nonsense can I acquire it. The world is mad after all. The only things that stands up to mad is nonsense. All I have to do is any one of those Kung Fu Ninja moves I see in the movies. It's not the move, he said. It's how much you believe it. It's ridiculous, but I have no choice but to try it. I run and imagine myself jumping in the air and kicking the Cheshire in the stomach.

Here I come with my None Fu powers.

I end up bumping into the Cheshire and falling again. None of what Jack promised me worked. I must be doing something wrong. Suddenly, I wonder why Jack's help doesn't appear to work. I mean, I'd go on a date with him now to save Constance.

"You really think you can try to stop me?" the Cheshire woman seems insulted by my attempt. She bends over me while I am on the floor, Constance choking in her grip. "Can't you see you're not the real Alice?" she says. "I have to admit, the Pillar had me fooled into believing it was you when you saved Constance in the Great Hall. This is why I invited you here, to see if you're the real Alice. But you're not. You have none of her strength. The real Alice is dead!"

The Cheshire keeps bending over me and grinning. I stretch my arm, hoping to find a stone to throw at him. I have succeeded in stalling him, but I have no idea what to do next. My hand comes across that useless umbrella again. I pull it near, knowing that it's not good enough to hit the Cheshire. All I do is point it at him to keep distance. I do it as if I am holding a gun. Wouldn't it be frabjous if this umbrella turned out to be a sword, like the one the White Queen had?

My hand accidentally pushes the umbrella's button and it springs open, separating me from the Cheshire who has already stretched back to suck Constance's soul. It all happens so fast, but the umbrella doesn't really block the view. It's rather transparent on my side, in the craziest way. I see coordinates and measurements all over it, as if it's a soldier's navigator.

Through the umbrella, I watch the Cheshire open Constance's mouth and start to inhale from it.

Suddenly, I realize there is a small trigger on my side of the umbrella. This little thing turns out to be one nonsensical gun. In a flash, I adjust the target on the Cheshire and pull the trigger.

If I was in my sane mind, I'd contemplate and try to find a meaning to all of this. But this is the mad world I am a living in. I watch as a surge of rainbow lightning hits the Cheshire like an electric current. The old woman falls on her knees. Not dead, but she lets Constance go and meows in pain.

I look at the umbrella in my hand in wonder. This is the silliest, most provocative weapon ever. I mean, it's even better than the Pillar's hookah.

The light gets the activists' attention. Seeing their tribal leader in pain, they let go of the Pillar and turn to me, all claws, all fangs, all mad.

I stand up and take Constance by the hand, running to the door leading down the stairs. The activists block the door and purr at me. I am a weakened human in Catland.

"If the umbrella is a gun, it must do other things too," the Pillar shouts. He is nodding at the cloistered windows while he's whipping at the activists with his hookah. I am not sure it's a good idea, but there is no way out and the Cheshire will be back on his feet soon. "Go on, Alice. I'll take care of these silly cats," the Pillar says.

I take a deep breath and run with Constance toward the window. No one stops me because there is nowhere for me to go. I stand on the edge and pull Constance up with me.

"What are you going to do, Alice?" Constance asks with horrified eyes, looking down at the massacre. It's too far below.

"You trust me, right?" I squeeze her hand. My other hand is holding the umbrella.

Constance nods and squeezes my hand back. "Are we going to jump?"

"Yes." My heart is racing. There is no other way out.

"You're like Mary Poppins."

"I don't know who that is. I have spent too much time in an asylum," I say. "Now, you are a brave girl and you will jump with me, right?"

She nods reluctantly.

"It's easy, Constance. All you have to do is believe."

"Believe in what, Alice?"

"Madness." I pull her tighter and jump.

Chapter 65

While people are getting killed below us, we float gently down to the ground with my umbrella. It's was easier than if I had had a parachute. Constance giggles at the magic. I pray to God that this is really happening and that I am not insane. While we land, cats fall from the sky all around us.

"The madness begins, Alice!" the Pillar shouts from above, before he gets back to his fight. I doubt he will survive this one.

But the Pillar is right. Landing with the umbrella is nothing compared to the madness happening around us. Big cats run after humans left and right, slashing at them and killing them. Many humans die because their minds can't comprehend the absurd reality of what's happening. When the sky rains cats, I believe it takes everyone some time to realize it's really happening.

I run with Constance next to me, shooting cats with my umbrella. I don't know if I should feel bad about it, but these aren't real cats. They are beasts made by the Cheshire. It's all wrong, but I promised a little girl that I would save her, and I am working on it. All I need is to bring her back to her parents. We run together through the narrow streets, wishing for the main road.

Out on the streets, Belgium police and ambulances are everywhere. But none of them want to take me and Constance. A nurse tells me that they figure we're alright and they better save the others. Seconds later, she gets bitten by one of the big cats.

I walk ahead and see that the whole massacre is being broadcasted on TV in the coffee shops already. People arc either appalled by it, or laughing their heads off. One boy asks if he can watch. He looks over my shoulder instead because he doesn't like this cartoon the grown-ups are watching.

Suddenly, a car rushes by, splashing dirt on us. Before I shout at the driver, he reverses, splashing me once more. I can't see him through the framed windows, but I don't need to be a magician to know who he is. It's an old cranky sports car, all white, and has diamonds painted all over it, making it look like one big silly playing card.

"Alice!" Jack Diamonds jumps out. "You're not stalking me, are you?" His dimples lower my guard again. The radio inside the car is playing a song called *It's Raining Cats, Hallelujah*.

"Seriously?" I pout. "It's you again?"

"I was attending a Formula One race in France," he says. "Just around the corner."

"And let me guess. You won, right?" I snicker.

"Actually, no. But I finished fourth," he says. "There were only four contestants. So what's all the fuss about the sky raining cats?" He looks over my shoulder.

"Believe me, you don't want to know."

"If you say so. How are you, Constance?" Jack says.

"I'm fine!" she giggles.

"Alice sure loves you," he says, kneeling down. "What kind of trouble did you get yourself into this time?"

"I was kidnapped by an old woman who thinks she is the Cheshire Cat," Constance replies.

"Did she have claws?" Jack says, his face dimming.

"Yes," Constance said. "How do you know?"

"I think she is actually coming for you again." Jack looks over Constance's shoulder.

I turn and see the Cheshire running in our direction. Constance clings to me again.

"I don't know what you guys got yourself into, but get in my car," Jack says. "Fast."

Chapter 66

Jack drives like a madman through the streets of Ypres.

"Seriously, how is that old woman moving so fast?" Jack glances in the rearview mirror.

"We're safe now," I say, sitting next to him, Constance in the back seat. "Thank you."

"Yes, thank you Jack." Constance says.

"Does that mean you're going out on a date with me?" he says.

"Not again," I sigh. "Why do you want to go on a date with me? I don't know you."

"Let's see. We've saved a girl together, fought a bunch of red-hooded monsters, and now escaped an old woman who thinks she is a cat. I've kissed girls before saying hello. You're practically my wife now. We even have kids," he winks at Constance in the back. Constance giggles.

"Okay," I sigh. "If you drive us safely back to Oxford."

"I will take you anywhere you want to go. Just ask, buttercup. So where and when? Are you free tonight?"

Suddenly, I am aware that I can't meet him at night and tell him so. I don't tell him I am in an asylum though. I don't think he'll like it. No one wants to date a girl with a Certificate of Insanity.

"So you have plans every night? What are you, a party animal?"

I laugh, thinking about my nightly parties with Waltraud and Ogier. "Let's just meet in daylight."

"So how is this going to be? The English way?"

"What do you mean?"

"I mean who's going to pay? English way, we split the check. American way, I pay the check. French way, probably you pay the check. Carrollian way, we eat mushrooms and drink tea in a house we break into."

"Wow, I didn't know you were this cheap."

"I am not cheap. I am broke. I stole the gas to drive this car to see you."

"So you admit you're stalking me."

"Well, yes. I am. I don't know what it is about you, but I can't stop thinking about you." He grips the stearing wheel, still speeding up.

My phone buzzes. I look at it as if I have totally forgotten about it. I haven't had one until two days ago anyways.

"Stop the car," I demand. "I need to take this call." I don't want him to hear me talk to the Pillar in case I have to mention something about the asylum. If I am going on a date with Jack, I want it to be as if I am just a normal girl.

"If you say so, buttercup." Jack complies and parks next to a grocery store. I get out and walk a few steps away to pick up the Pillar's call.

"Where are you?" the Pillar says.

"On my way back to Oxford," I don't want him to know I am with Jack. He will keep telling me he is a distraction. "I have Constance. Are you alright?"

"I had to play woof woof with the activists for a while, but I am," he says. "I think from now on there will be no more Kattenstoet Festival. I spattered a lot of cat blood on the wall. The whole tower is pretty much jinxed. But the Cheshire escaped."

"Yes, I know. He was just after us but we..."

Before I finish my sentence, Jack's car gets hit by a big yellow school bus. The phone flies in the air and smashes into pieces. I turn to look for Jack. He is drowning in his blood. My eyes shift to the back seat. Constance isn't there. When I raise my head, I see the Cheshire driving the schools bus. He isn't wearing the mask, still in his woman form. He has Constance pulled by her hair next to him. When I look for my umbrella to shoot him again, I discover that I am bleeding, too dizzy from the hit. I fall to the asphalt, spiraling down into my own personal darkness.

Part Three:
We're All Mad Everywhere

Chapter 67

Quadrangle, Christ Church, Oxford University

When I wake up, I am sitting on a bank next to the fountain in the middle of the garden of Christ Church College. The snow is still covering most of the ground around me. I feel like my wound has been medically mended, and it's only been a couple of hours or so. The sun has winked and the twilight of evening has passed. It's nighttime.

"It's been a long day," the Pillar says. He's sitting next to me on the bank on his can, like always.

"Why am I here?" I say. "Shouldn't I be back in the asylum by now?"

"I am surprised this is the first question you ask," the Pillar remarks. "I thought you'd ask about Constance."

"Why would I?" I am fighting the tears in my eyes. "I am a failure. And it's all because of you." I know I'm not being reasonable, laying all fault on him. "You keep believing that I am the real Alice, when I am just a mad girl in an asylum."

"Which makes me think," he says, unaffected by my blaming. "What's more important for you now: to know if you're the real Alice, or to know who you really are and what you're capable of."

"I'm fed up with your riddles," I say. "I'm fed up with the sane world. I want to go back to my cell where I belong. It's easier to be insane, than live with the guilt of giving up on Constance."

"You know what insane people are, Alice?" the Pillar says. "They are just sane people who know too much."

"I tried all I can. Whenever I think I've saved Constance, the Cheshire gets her back. I bet he has sucked her soul already and regained his powers." I am about to stand up. Listening to him has messed with my head.

"No, he hasn't," the Pillar waves the Cheshire's mask in his hand. "I stole the mask from him when I was in the clothes tower. He wants it back."

"He contacted you?"

"Yes. He wants to exchange Constance for the mask."

"But what use is the mask without Constance and the festival?" I wonder.

"He has sucked Constance's soul already and the ritual was technically a success," the Pillar explains. "It turns out that the other girls died when he sucked their souls because they weren't the *one*. Constance had like an extra soul for him inside. Whatever magic Lewis used, he made sure she'd still live if the Cheshire got his soul back. Sucking it didn't get her killed. He has no use for her now."

"So all he needs is the mask?" My face lights up. "What are we waiting for? Let's give him the mask and get Constance."

"It's not that easy, Alice. You must realize the danger he will bring onto the world once he has restored his power. He will simply be unstoppable, and will start opening the doors to the Wonderland Monsters. I wouldn't be surprised if he releases the Mad Hatter and the others soon."

"But Constance..."

"This is where it gets complicated," he says, still looking at the Tom Tower ahead. "You see, I could have just burned this mask and the Cheshire's grin with it, but I didn't. I wanted to give you a choice. I still believe you're the real Alice, and will trust your decision."

"You keep believing in me while no one else does," I sigh. "I wonder why."

"I'm mad enough to believe in you, that's all," the Pillar says. "The world is too sane. It could use a little madness."

"So either I let Constance die and save the world from the Wonderland Monsters, or I save Constance and doom the world," I say. "Who am I to make a decision like that?"

"I am sure your decision will be much better than the likes of Margaret Kent and all those politicians who suck away our lives like cats do to an infant. Every day, they make decisions that end up becoming tangles in wars. My hope is that you will make the right decision though," the Pillar turns to face me. "I know someone who can help you decide."

"It's not your chauffeur, is it?"

"Of course not. He has the wisdom of rats, which means his answer to almost everything is 'cheese.'" the Pillar says. "You see the Tom Tower?" He nods at it. "I killed someone in it in the past. I messed with his mind and made him jump off of it."

"I'm not in the mood to listen to your--"

"The Tom Tower has the answer, Alice," he cuts me off. "Remember when I told you that its bell rings 101 times at 9:00 PM, Oxford time?"

"You told me more than once," I gaze up at the magnificent construction.

"It's five minutes to nine," the Pillar says. "It will ring five minutes from now. If you climb up, you will find a small door on the northern wall. It's hidden behind an armoire. Just move it and you will find it."

"A door?"

"Remember that you have to be back before the 101 dongs, or you'll be lost behind it forever."

"What's behind the door?" I am already standing up, curious for anything that helps me decide. "A treasure?" I mock him.

The Pillar leans back. "No. The doors in this University are much more precious than that. It's a door to one of your memories."

Chapter 68

Tom Tower, Christ Church, Oxford University

It doesn't take me long to find the door in Tom Tower. I kneel down to open it. All I can think of is Alice in the books. Wouldn't it be cool if I had eaten something that would make me shrink, instead of crawling through on my knees?

There is an endless white light behind the door. It only disappears with the Tom Tower's first dong.

I walk farther and find myself in the same place on Tom Quad's roof, a hundred and fifty years ago. I am standing in a room. It looks like a studio. It's filled with all kinds of art, drawings, and photographs. It's nighttime. It's summertime. I come across one of the 19th-century cameras. There is also a big table full of photographs of young girls. They are old photographs, in black and white and sometimes in sepia. Most of them are of a girl who looks a lot like me.

I rummage through the photographs and find many other photos of other girls. Names and dates are scribbled on the back. It's apparent there is a significant purpose for these photos. There are charts, maps, and writings annexed to them. I have no time to read them all.

I come by Alice Constance Westmaccott's photo. She looks almost like the Constance I know in real life. I flip the photo and read it:

"Daughter of Richard Westmaccott. Remember to ask him which one is the real mask with the cat's grin."

This must be Lewis Carroll's handwriting. I am in his studio in Oxford University.

A little further down it says: "I think the Red Queen was right. The Cheshire can't be beheaded because he keeps appearing and disappearing. The only way is to steal his grin. It's got his power."

I hear sounds down in Christ Church's garden. When I look over I glimpse someone running, but I miss them. I climb down and follow them to the Great Hall.

Inside, I come across the fireplace with the firedogs. It's not a fireplace yet, but a door leading somewhere. The door is closed, but is shimmering with golden light underneath. It shakes to thuds and the sound of fighting. There are screams. I don't know what to do. It's like a war going on behind it. I wonder if Wonderland is behind that door.

Finally, the door springs open. A young man comes out. He is wearing a black priest's outfit and holds the vorpal sword in his hand, the same sword I saw the White Queen holding. He locks the door behind him with a golden key that he hangs around his head after. He is panting from the struggle behind the door. The man has that aura that makes me love him at first sight. It's the same kind of love I felt toward the White Queen. I realize what it is now. It's love shared by those who walk the white tiles on the chessboard of life.

"Alice?" he wonders, still catching his breath. "What are you doing here?" He is stuttering. A small white rabbit peeks out of his pocket, nibbling on a carrot. It's a funny looking rabbit. "Alice?" It imitates the man. "What are you doing here?"

"You see me?" I am bedazzled.

Lewis Carroll laughs. It's a delightful laugh. A laugh of someone who has not lost his childhood to the burden of growing up. I like it a lot. I only wonder why he stutters. "I see you," he says and tucks his hand gently back into his pocket. He takes my hand after. From his touch and my height, I realize I am seven years old, probably dressed in a blue dress. I still avoid mirrors wherever I go.

We walk outside and sit on the same bank I sat on with the Pillar.

"I did it, Alice," Lewis says. "I locked them up."

"The Wonderland Monsters?"

"If you'd like to call them that, yes."

"Is that the door to Wonderland?" I ask him, thinking about the fireplace in real life. It was walled up by bricks.

"One of many," he says. "I trapped the monsters behind each of the doors. They are interlinked, but they can only crossover to the world from the same door where I trapped them."

"And the Cheshire?"

"He is the only one I couldn't get, but I stole his grin," he says. "I hid it the best way I could."

"Oh," I say. I wonder what happens if I tell him I am from the future.

"Are you alright?" He holds my face gently in his hands. I nod. His cold hands feel warm on my cheeks. "I am so sorry, Alice. It's all my fault, but I didn't know things would turn out this way." I don't understand why he is sorry, and I am aware of Tom Tower dinging in the distance. I don't think he can hear it. "Here," he takes off the necklace with the key and wraps it around my neck. "This is one of six keys needed to open each door to Wonderland, where I locked them all in. I trust you can keep this one safe."

The key glitters in gold around my neck. I realize it's the same key drawn on my cell's wall.

"Lewis," I ask. "What happens on January 14th?"

"Fourteenth?" he wonders. "I have no idea. Why?"

"Doesn't matter," I don't have time to tell him about my cell. The Pillar sent me here so Lewis could help me with my decision. "I need you to help me decide something."

"I hope I can." he says.

"If it comes down to saving one girl's life and saving the world, who should I choose?"

"You started saving lives already? I always knew you would," his smile curves like ocean waves I want to crash against. "You really want my opinion on this?"

"You really want his opinion?" The carrot-nibbling rabbit peeks out again. Lewis laughs, hands him another carrot, and tucks him back in his suit pocket. The rabbit stretches its arm out of Lewis's hand pocket, "It takes too much space in here."

Lewis laughs again then turns to me. "Like I said, do you really want my opinion?"

I nod.

"In my opinion, no one can save the world, Alice," he says. "We can save the ones we care about, the ones nearby, if we're lucky enough to be able to save them in the first place. Then once we save one, we go on to the next. One day at a time, Alice. One day at a time."

"So there are no miracles like saving the world?"

Lewis laughs. "There are two ways to live our lives, Alice. One is as though nothing is a miracle. The other is as though everything is a miracle. I like the 'everything' part."

"I like it too," I say.

"A man called Einstein will rephrase this quote many years from now, by the way," Lewis stands up and cleans his sword. "Don't tell him I said it before him. We don't want to shake his confidence."

"Why?"

"He is going to invent mad things, important things for mankind, and no one's going to believe him in the beginning," Lewis says. "That's the way with all mad people. No one believes them in the beginning."

I pull him down and kiss him on the cheek. He blushes. "You're a good man, Lewis. The world will love your madness after you die."

"You think so?"

"Your book is going to inspire millions, believe me," I say, and run back to the Tom Tower.

"What book, Alice?" he summons after me. "Wait? I am going to write a book? About what?"

"If you know about Einstein quoting you years from now, you should know you're going to write a book." I don't turn around, but answer him as I run.

"A book?" I hear the rabbit question. "Lewis, you're going to write a book? Will you write about me, please?"

"A book about what, Alice?" are Lewis's last words I hear before I reach the Tom Tower.

"Madness, Lewis. You're going to write a book about beautiful madness."

Chapter 69

Quadrangle, Christ Church, Oxford University

I stand in the middle of Christ Church's quadrangle with the Cheshire's mask in my hand. There a few students here and there, a couple of professors, and even a mother and her little child with a lollipop in her hand. I think this is a night gathering for some reason. None of it concerns me. I am here to give the Cheshire his mask and get Constance back.

The Cheshire doesn't waste time. It's only moments before I see the old woman before me.

"I believe you have something that was stolen from me," she says.

"Where is Constance?" I say.

"With her parents. I drove her myself and they invited me for ice cream before I left," the woman grins. "Call the Pillar to make sure."

I do. The Pillar replies with a yes. I ask him to put Constance on the phone because I don't trust him. When she talks to me, I ask her about who she thought I was before jumping from the clothes tower. She says, "Mary Poppins." Now, I am sure it's her.

"Here is your stupid grin," I hand him the mask.

The woman puts on the mask immediately. This time it dissolves into the pores of her face, like soap. She closes her eyes for a brief time, then opens them with the creepiest grin ever on her face. I can tell this is the Cheshire's real grin. It's not something you want to stare at for too long, or it will suck your soul.

"This feels good," the woman says. "If I were you, I would start the countdown."

"To what?"

"The end of the world, dear Alice," the woman's grin has turned permanent. "You don't think I had my revenge yet, do you?" She tickles my chin with her finger and walks away. I feel helpless. Although I saved Constance, I just booked the world a First Class ticket to Hell.

"Nine lives aren't that hard to kill," I say over my shoulder. She stops. "I know who I am now, and I will kill you nine times if I have to."

"With what, your magic pink umbrella?" The woman turns around and approaches me again. "Do you really want to see a glimpse of the grandness of my power?" She doesn't wait for an answer and gestures at a young man walking by. She taps him on the shoulder and suddenly the man turns to me with her grin on his face.

"How do you like me now, Alice?" the young man asks me in his male voice. He waves at his girlfriend and she approaches him. They kiss. Once they do, the grin transfers to her. "How about now, Alice?" the young girl grins at me. She leaves her boyfriend and I follow her through the grounds, where she helps an old man find his wallet. Once she touches him, he becomes the new Cheshire. "And how about now, Alice?" the old man says. He drops his wallet again and the kid with the lollipop hurries and brings it to him. It's only a second before she has the grin on her face. "Do you like lollipops, Alice?" She offers me hers.

I stand paralyzed. Now I know why Lewis couldn't catch the Cheshire, why his power was the most evil power in the world. The Cheshire was no one, yet everyone. It was like spreading evil through the world by the touch of a hand. I watch the girl kneel down and pet a stray cat. The grin transfers to the cat. She meows at me and runs through the crowd. I trail after her. Wherever I look, someone has the grin for a brief moment.

I stand in the middle of the quadrangle, feeling lost. There is nothing I could ever do to catch the Cheshire.

Chapter 70

The Pillar lays on his back on the couch. He is still smoking and listening to Alice in the Sky with Diamonds. The butterfly in the jar is calmer now. It doesn't push her way out of the glass. I am too exhausted to be here, but thought I'd tell him that I am ready for the job. I am ready to save lives.

"I see the butterfly is calmer now," I remark.

"I had to send her some of my hookah smoke to ease her," he says.

"I wonder why you keep her."

"I am a caterpillar, Alice," he chortles. "One day I am going to be as beautiful as her. She helps me remember this."

"Whatever," I don't have the strength for another riddle. "I'm here to tell you that I'm..."

"Ready to save lives?"

"Yes."

"Ready to accept that you're Alice, even if it makes no sense?"

"Yes."

"Ready for accepting the madness in your life?"

"Yes." I am reluctant about this part.

"How about the None Fu techniques? Did you master those?"

"Not at all," I laugh. "I tried it, and it doesn't work. It's such nonsense. How is Jack by the way?"

"We went on a date together. It was a Carrollian date, where neither of us paid because we snuck into the restaurant when it was rather late. He tried to kiss me, but he smelled of playing cards. I'm not going out with him again." He doesn't even catch his breath when he jokes like this.

"It means you haven't seen him," I say. "And he is hard to track. With all his nonsense, I was warming up to him. I mean, he is a stalker, but he just wanted a date with a mad and lonely girl like me. What more could I ask for? I hope he is alright."

"I am sure he will be," the Pillar says, "You should get some sleep. Now that the Cheshire is on the loose, I wouldn't be surprised if you and I are invited to a tea party in a few days."

"In the Parliament, I imagine?"

"Or the Queen of England's palace," he tops my mockery. "You haven't discovered who the Red Queen is and why she always said, 'off with their heads' yet."

"Please," I raise a hand. "Enough for today. I don't want to know. You're right. I have to get some sleep."

"How was the meeting with Carroll?" he catches up before I go. "Did he give you anything, if I may ask?"

"Not at all. He just advised me to save Constance," I am feeling the key Lewis gave me in my pocket. I am not going to tell the Pillar about it. I feel the Pillar shouldn't know these things. "Since you have a writing desk in your cell, aren't you going to tell me what a raven and a writing desk have in common?"

The Pillar turns his head toward me and smiles. He knows I am changing the subject, like he always does. "Not now. But I could let you ponder over an even crazier question, one that historians always skip and never investigate thoroughly."

"Oh, and what would that be?"

"What does Lewis Carroll and Red Riding Hood have in common?" he says.

"What? Are you crazy? Of course they have nothing in common." I roll my eyes and begin to walk. "I never thought I'd say goodnight to a serial killer, but goodnight Professor Pillar."

"One more thing, Alice," he stops me. "There is something that still puzzles me."

"Puzzles you?" I raise an eyebrow.

"In the previous days, you have never tried to look up your bus accident, neither on the Internet or anywhere else," he says. "I wonder why that is."

"I don't know," I reply. "I guess I was busy."

"Unlikely."

"Maybe I am just not ready to see the faces of the friends I killed. Adam told me something like that in my dream."

"Oh," he drags from his pipe. "That's most likely it."

He turns off the lights and disappears in the dark.

Chapter 71

Alice's Cell, Radcliffe Asylum

In my cell, I put my umbrella next to my Tiger Lily and prepare to sleep. Waltraud tells me there is no shock therapy today. She thinks Ogier went overboard last time, and I ended up hallucinating. I don't even try to understand why she doesn't believe me.

When I enter the cell, Waltraud doesn't lock the door behind me. Before I check out the reason, I am surprised to see I have a visitor in my cell.

"Fabiola?" I wonder. "I mean, White Queen?"

"How have you been, Alice?" she smiles serenely as usual. "I thought I'd surprise you."

"How did you get in?"

Her smile widened. It was like telling me she could do a lot of things like this.

"I am honored by your visit, anyways."

"I see the umbrella was useful," she says.

"Very useful. Thank you," I say. "May I ask where you got it?"

"It's one of Lewis Carroll's gadgets," the White Queen laughed. "He invented many of those later in his life. He even invented martial arts of his own. It's called None Fu."

"So I have been told," I roll my eyes. "Does it work?"

"Not with everyone," she replies. "I came to tell you something, Alice."

"All ears, Fabiola." I lower my head.

"Remember when I told you you're not Alice?"

I nod.

"I lied," she says. "I know a woman in my position shouldn't lie, but this was...a white lie."

"Why did you lie?"

"The truth is, I am still not sure if you're the Alice, but I am also not sure you're not."

"Can't you tell by my looks?"

"That's a tricky thing. Before we left Wonderland, Lewis made us drink a potion that would make us forget your face," she sighs.

"Why?"

"He wanted to protect you in case the Wonderland Monsters escaped and we'd need you again. He cared a great deal for you," the White Queen said. "I heard you did brave things in the last couple of days." She smiles the way Lewis smiled at me. "I am proud of you, whether you're the real Alice or not."

"Thank you Fabiola. That means a lot to me."

"This is why I brought you a present," she pulls out a hand mirror. I back off immediately. "Don't be afraid. I am not going to let anything hurt you. But if you want to take that route of saving lives, you need to take one brief look at it."

"Why, Fabiola? You know I have a mirror phobia."

"There is a reason why you have it, Alice," Fabiola says. "Mirrors show truth sometimes. Your mind is suppressing one, and it's my job to show it to you, so you know where you stand. A strong and brave heart isn't enough. A true heart, no matter how much the truth hurts, is the strongest of all."

"You think I really should?"

"Do you know what the name 'Alice' means? It means 'the truth.' Whether you want to know or not, that's your choice." She lays the mirror on the floor. "It's going to be a hurtful memory, but you need it. Sometimes truth comes along with a little pain. The pain will subside eventually, and the truth shall remain. See you soon, little hero," she tells me, and walks out the door. She doesn't walk out through the wall or anything. Just the cell's door, which she shuts from the outside.

She leaves me trapped with a mirror in my room.

Chapter 72

Waltraud enters my cell some time later. I find myself waking up. I must have slept after the White Queen's visit. Waltraud puts a plate of food next to me. It's a bigger and much healthier portion than before. I wonder if that's the Pillar's effect.

"So was it you who let the White Queen in?"

"What White Queen?" Waltraud drags on her cigarette.

"I mean Fabiola."

"Who's Fabiola?" Waltraud looks irritated with me.

"The nun," I grimace.

"There was no nun," Waltraud says. "No one entered your room after I brought you here, Alice. What are you talking about?"

"Don't keep playing those games with me, Waltraud." I feel my anger surfacing. "First you pretend you didn't see me on TV, and then this. Why are you doing this?"

Waltraud laughs. "Your situation is getting worse. I am reporting it to Dr. Truckle."

"What is wrong with you?" I snap. "Why do you want me to feel this way? Can't you see the Tiger Lily isn't responding to me? I am not hallucinating."

"The flower never responded to you in the first place," Waltraud doesn't stop laughing. My misery is her entertainment. "Why would a non-responding flower be a sign of sanity? It's all in your head, Alice."

"No, it's not," I pull the umbrella and open it. "Look at this crazy umbrella. It has a screen in it." I pull it open, but don't see any of the navigational tools. There is no trigger to pull. I can't believe this." I turn and face Waltraud. "You have to believe me. I am the real Alice. I saved a life today."

"You're just a mad girl in an asylum underground," Waltraud keeps laughing, about to close the door. "Maybe that's what Lewis Carroll meant by Alice's Adventures *Under Ground*." Her laugh echoes behind the door she slams. "You know that's the book's originally title, don't you?"

Chapter 73

I decide that I have no choice but to look in the mirror. I'm not mad. I know I'm not mad.

At first, I don't see anything in the mirror. I discover it's covered with dust, so I wipe it clean. I hold it in my hand, thinking I could just crack it if the rabbit shows up.

The mirror shows me standing at a bus stop, waiting for a friend. I am about seventeen, and I am holding a boy's hand. It's Adam again, still wearing his hood. Friends arrive and start to behave just like in my older dream of killing them all in the end.

I don't know why I am seeing this, but I keep watching.

We get on the bus, everyone jokes, and I am suspicious of the driver. It's the rabbit again. I can't help it and go grab the wheel, trying to save the bus.

"No, Alice," Adam screams from under the hood. "Don't do it." He still thinks it's me who kills everyone on the bus. Well, maybe it was me. I am not sure.

Suddenly, Adam pulls his hood back.

It's the heart-shattering moment. It's that moment when I see his face. I let go of the wheel, not knowing what to think. The boy under the hood is Jack Diamonds.

If you switch the letters in Jack Diamonds you get Adam J Dixon, bearing in mind that the 'x' letter in Dixon is translated as the letters 'c', 'k' and 's' in Jack Diamonds. My mind must have come up with this trick to escape the horrible truth that I killed Adam in the schools bus.

At the end of the memory, the rabbit in the mirror appears. He parts the hair dangling in front of him and I discover it's me underneath. It's always been me.

I sink to my knees and let the mirror fall, splintering into pieces. I don't know what's real and what's not. I don't know why I killed those people on the bus. Did I make up Jack's personality? Was it all in my mind? But how is that possible? How did he save me so many times? Or is it like Waltraud said, that I have never left the ward underground and that it was all in my head?

I stand up and hold the bars in the door's window and start screaming. "I'm not mad," I plead. I pound on the door, but no one answers me. Why would they? I am just a mad girl in an asylum underground. "Who in the world am I?" I mumble, staring at the long ward. It seems endless from where I stand. I need to get out to prove I am not mad. I need to go meet the Pillar. He can't be an illusion of my mind. I don't know how long I can't wait. I am dying here.

Ogier approaches my cell slowly when I don't stop screaming. The hallway is dark, but I recognize him from his white shaved head. "I told you we're all mad here, Alice," he says, and my confusion peaks. Why would Ogier say that?

I only get it when his face shines through the dim light coming from my cell. He stands behind the barred window in my door, and it all makes sense now. He is the Cheshire. I recognize him from his grin. "Now if you'll excuse me, I have a world to apocalypse." He looks at me for a moment and turns around, whistling as he leaves the ward. As he leaves, I hear him hum the nursery rhyme:

When she was sane, she was very, very sane. And when she was mad, she was Alice.

The END...

Want to read the next part of Alice's story?

Just visit: www.Cameronjace.com and enter your email. You'll get personal updates from me. (totally spam free) I promise you'll be the first to know when Book Two is released! (Coming October 30 2014, basically titled: Insanity 2!) Also, you will know about the facts behind the book and how places like the Kattenstoet festival look. I will post details, photos, and addresses about the crazy world behind Alice in Wonderland.

So don't miss out: www.cameronjace.com

Or follow me on Facebook: http://www.facebook.com/camjace

Thank you so much for reading.

Love all the monsters,

Cameron Jace

Made in the USA
San Bernardino, CA
21 November 2016